T0284471

Affirmation of Poetry   **Judith Balso**

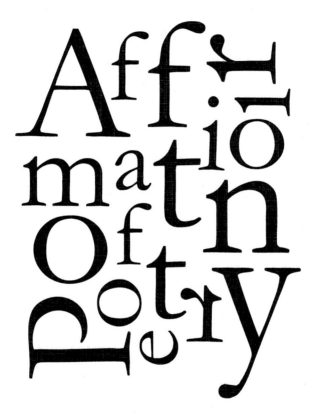

Translated by Drew S. Burk   Univocal

Affirmation de la poésie
by Judith Balso
© NOUS, 2011

Translated by Drew S. Burk
as *Affirmation of Poetry*
First Edition
Minneapolis © 2014, Univocal Publishing

Published by Univocal
123 North 3rd Street, #202
Minneapolis, MN 55401

Designed & Printed by Jason Wagner

Distributed by the University of Minnesota Press

ISBN 9781937561178
Library of Congress Control Number 2014942540

Table of Contents

Translator's Note

In the following translation, I have respected Judith Balso's style by re-translating poems and using citations sparingly. When footnotes do appear, it is to cite an existing translation that was used; in some cases, I have consulted existing translations but nevertheless altered them in accordance with the author's French versions to remain as close as possible to her thought. For the cited poems of Alberto Caeiro, I have consulted the existing translations of Edwin Honig and Chris Daniels. Unless otherwise noted, I re-translated the poems referenced in the following work except for Wallace Stevens' poems, which were originally written in English. While Judith Balso doesn't provide numerous citations, she offers a listing of sources used in the following work as well as a list of her other writings that can be found at the end of the book.

I would like to thank Lucca Fraser for her help translating an early draft of chapter 7. I would also like to thank Judith Balso for her advice and counsel during the final stages of preparing the translation of this work.

- Drew S. Burk

To Ginou,
whose death wounded this book

I read poets, I learn from poets. The idea for this small book came to me at a time when I felt the possibility of a global (and by this I don't mean "general") declaration regarding the power of poetic work: regarding the immense reservoir that it constitutes and which has, as of yet, hardly been truly explored.

I do not share the diagnosis that there is a contemporary deterioration of poetry. The work of the poets continues; it is neither more nor less besieged than that of the true theater or an inventive politics that is not beholden to a party affiliation. It takes place. Despite those powers striving to deny the point, the world is a thought-world.

I will organize this declaration around four inquiries which have as their aim to affirm the importance of poetry for thought:

- What part of this thought-world is constructed, when Bei Dao, among others, proposes that poetry is the capacity for cold indifference [*froideur*] – "to withdraw oneself from all passions and impulses" – the capacity for distancing itself from pathos, the capacity of "indirectly" saying it – because "directly" saying it is too simple?"

- Why does Chen Dong Dong – quoting William Carlos Williams – make the following remark? "If we want a new verse to appear, we must have confidence in the birth of a new thought." By placing his thought next to that of Paul Celan, according to whom "the primary function of any poetry [is] to be purely and simply available" (from an introductory note to a selection of German translations of the poems of Osip Mandelstam), seems to me to reveal a renewed thinking of poetry as thought.

- How do we navigate between the appropriate reduction of language enunciated by Bei Dao (which I will make speak once again regarding this point as an echo):

> Many languages
> Fly through this world
> But the production of language
> Can neither increase nor diminish
> The silent pain of humanity

and the conviction that poetry operates in a profound manner, in opening up the imagination, in displacing naming, in upsetting not only our way of speaking but our way of thinking?

- And finally – though it will not be a conclusion – why does Wallace Stevens make the following utterance (in "The Man with the Blue Guitar"):

> Poetry is the subject of the poem
> From this the poem issues
> And to this returns

which seems to me to be a principle of the utmost amplitude, in no way being a closing in on itself, of the poem?

By way of a prologue

Kleist, "Letter from one poet to another:"

"Language, rhythm, assonances, however seductive they may be, above all if they are a type of ornamental covering for the spirit, considered from this point of view, are no less (in and of themselves) an *authentic disadvantage*, even if it is necessary and fatal; *and art can only bear the function to eliminate it as much as possible*. I use the best of my abilities attempting to provide clarity to expression, significa-tion to meter, grace and life to the musicality of words: not in order to place value upon these things, but *in order for the idea contained within them to be able to make itself manifest*. Because the quality of any authentic form is to allow for the instantaneous emergence without mediation of the spirit, whereas the imperfect form, like a bad mirror, *holds it captive, without suggesting anything else other than itself.*"

I would like to place this book under the sign of Kleist. In first meditating on these lines in which I would like to emphasize the motif of a radical distrust of the poet vis-à-vis language: a motif which continues today to the point of making poets the strongest antithesis of the communicative world presented to us as the lone real.

Under the sign of Kleist I would also like to place the pro-cess (which in my opinion is entirely poetic) by which, in the last newspaper he published, Kleist knew how to use the policing constraint, that was imposed upon him by censure, against itself, in order to make the most subtle and percussive use of it to un-derscore the censure and circumvent it. In a Prussia occupied by Napoleon's army, and in order to palliate the miserable situation of the Berlin press (reduced to only two newspapers that appeared three times a week), in the autumn of 1810, Kleist sets about creating a Berlin evening newspaper called the *Berliner Abendblätter* with Adam Müller.

The newspaper was concerned with making a theatrical play out of the lies and propaganda deployed within the occupied territory by the French newspapers, *Le Moniteur* and *Le Journal de Paris*. Kleist had already published a pamphlet called, *Manual of French Journalism* in which he stated all the "good things" he thought of these newspapers. Among other things, the pamphlet contained the following definition: "French journalism is the art of making the people believe what the government believes it appropriate for them to believe" — a definition which he counters with: "In general, journalism represents the simple and direct manner of informing the people of what is happening in the world. It is an entirely private activity, and the objectives of the government, whatever their designation may be, are foreign to this practice."

And here we find the constraint: I deliberately use the word constraint because Kleist plagiarized the OULIPO by anticipation, using the police laws precisely in the sense of an Oulipean constraint. I provide you with this constraint in the same terms in which Kleist began inserting them, and thus made them known to his readers as such in his first *Berliner Abendblatt*:

> An order from the Royal prefect of police, M. Gruner, who supports any enterprise of public interest with as much kindness as goodwill, leads us to the obligation of inserting into this special edition, as well as the edition we are publishing today, *any article concerning extraordinary events or representing an interest from the point of view of the police*, which has recently taken place in the city or its outskirts: *these articles must not omit any detail, they must be thorough and credible*; in such a way that the pages we are adding to the principal content, and which we hope will enrich the contents thanks to statistical information coming from the region, will constitute not only a permanent chronicle of the city of Berlin but the entire kingdom of Prussia.

What we see ensue is Kleist's plan to put into place, for the readers of his newspaper, what we could call a "dual agreement:" under the guise of publishing what the police ask him to, Kleist will construct a way that, any reader who would care to do so, can in reality, be instructed on what is rotten in the kingdom of Prussia.

Kleist begins by conscientiously reproducing excerpts from four police reports, each speaking of unexplained fires in Berlin and the surrounding areas, fires that seemed to be aimed at specific houses, being either a public inn or the property of a public figure. The editorial staff of the newspaper specifies the belongings of a lodger or the public figure had been found in the hands of a vagabond and insidiously insinuates: "This leaves us the hope of being able to retrace the steps of the individuals who are really at the origin of the majority of the fires. (As soon as the editorial staff is notified by the superior authority of the police of this happy news the staff will make it known to the public, in order to reassure it.) It is the kind of report that has the effect of further compounding the feeling that has already been created by the list of mysterious fires, indicating that grave unrest continues without the police having any mastery over it whatsoever. We should add that in Prussia the news propaganda of the mysterious fires inevitably recalls memories of the unrest during the Peasants' War. The published police report will startle those who know Kleist's work: as with the whole story of the *Prince of Homburg* (which Kleist will write in 1811), this report indeed pivots around a story of a *glove*. It was found in the middle of the street and handed over to the police, "an old cotton glove" having belonged to a military surgeon containing "several cinders and a prepared bundle of charcoal soaked in alcohol intended to spark a fire once it has encountered a flame."

All the documents issued by the police are presented in a way so as to magnify the agonizing nature of the reports. For example, under the guise of "providing several details regarding the fire starter named Schwarz and the band of hoodlums he was a part of," Kleist reports, in a conclusion as good as any found in a horror novel, that "the investigation has shown that each member of this organization knows how to counterfeit his profile, is capable of adopting various disguises, successively borrowing names, and playing various roles, according to the circumstances. All of them know how to falsify passports, photo I.D.s, signatures, and the individual Grabowsky who appears in the protocol under the number 2, is a virtuoso in the art of confectioning and

13

fastening seals and stamps." Every concrete detail serves to establish the resemblance of fantasy of the "organized group" ("organized group" not being a phrase borne from the persecutory governmental policing of the current French government).

The editorial staff does not object in the slightest to the government's excellent intentions:

> We report for example, threatening letters or flammable materials have been discovered, fires have been lit for which we have yet to find the authors. It goes without saying that our intention is not to elicit public apprehension, whereas, even if no declaration whatsoever has expressly been made in regard to this subject, all possible measures have been taken by the authorities to prevent further crimes, and they continue to be on the lookout for the authors; on the contrary what is necessary is to denounce the rumors that see 100 threatening letters when in reality there is merely one, which thus contributes to the propagation of fear and horror among worried minds.

The newspaper then interrupts this thread to throw itself headlong into an obscure history of an errant dog that goes to battle against the dogs of an alderman; leading to the animal being declared rabid and thus shot, along with the dogs of the alderman for good measure. Elsewhere, another dog, an "evil dog" is said to have bitten both "humans and animals." In truth, this second dog did not bite anyone at all, save for perhaps several other dogs, some of which were shot and others put under observation. Nevertheless, as the so called evil dog had "kindly agreed to leave, it is more than likely, the article concludes, that he wasn't rabid at all."

Kleist proposes a small apologue toward the wisdom of everyone: regarding rumors and the possible gravity of their consequences – here we have dogs that are shot for having done nothing. The following edition of the newspaper must appeal to the category of "erratum" in order to conceal the fact that the text from the morning (presented here as a "report concerning the subject of an evil dog") did not, properly speaking, constitute a police report and that its "onus falls exclusively upon the editorial staff."

Kleist then explores the beneficial resources comprised via the publication of a "disclaimer": a French courier freshly arrived in Berlin would have "denied" the "chatter which indicated the French troops had wiped out the setbacks in Portugal." Publishing a disclaimer is an occasion to spread the inverse chatter, which would be good news for those opposing the Napoleonic occupation of Prussia.

The newspaper closes the series with a final article recounting the story of how a regular soldier refused to obey the orders of his commanding officer, and while the commanding officer wanted to put the soldier in a detention cell, the soldier ended up putting a bullet in the officer's head. A news story that says quite a bit about the state of military discipline within the army, corrupted by its collaboration with the occupying forces.

So it is that Kleist magnificently takes advantage of the initial constraint: in excessively "informing" his readers, in using and exaggerating each detail, as well as theatrically staging the functioning of rumors; he uses the constraint of the police reports so well that the police cannot say anything about it. The pure poetic work, using merely the police materials, is capable of producing the possibility of dual effects and thus of dual understandings.

Police literature – the literature of "reports" – is imperceptibly turned into fiction, just enough to allow for the power of the real to emerge.

That a tragic poet of Kleist's magnitude invented such an apparatus that both flaunted and evaded the constraint of the police, in my opinion, shows a profound knowledge regarding both the police and poetry respectively.

Developing Kleist's extraordinary poetic use of the newspaper could seem to be incongruous here, but it justifies itself via several motifs: this invention is exemplary for my discussion which will support the idea that the singular greatness of poetic work is that it conceives itself as fiction which thinks itself as a fiction, and it does this without having its sights set toward skeptical or nihilistic ends, but according to a principle of affirmation and truth. In the work of Kleist: it is also a principle of combat.

To me, it seems that this incident found in the *Abendblätter* helps in understanding how the poetic work of fictioning is the immanent capacity to produce truths, from the interior of a limit and a constraint that are always those of language. Here we are not talking about poems in the proper sense, but the poetic

15

capacity to bypass the language of the police, which is merely a particularly striking example.

With this extreme example, we are also talking about what I propose calling "poetic events," and which constitutes my principle for reading poets and poems. One of the objectives of this book is to encourage you to share this principle.

Events of thought whose site is comprised of one or several poems, or better still a poetic configuration constituted by the works of several poets, are what I name "poetic events." I will immediately add that these poetic events are multiple and absolutely varied. I mention this from the very beginning to indicate that I am far from accepting the idea of foundations or general utterances such as "the poem is the site of being" or "the poem as the site of presence," that would reduce the poem to a single thread.

It is a question of entering into poems via another door rather than the already existing ones, which in my eyes are not enough: history, schools, periods, forms, current situations, countries, writings, or styles....

In order to provide a way to measure the magnitude and the extent of what I mean by poetic events, I have chosen to name and present seven such examples:

1. Wallace Stevens takes the sun back from Plato in order to no longer make a figure of Idea out of it, but to expose it as a figure of appearance [*apparaitre*] – "*the seeming,*"[1] that I propose writing "*appar-être*," in French – a figure which cannot bear a name.

2. Alberto Caeiro invents a surprising poem of "seeing," at the limits of prose, breaking with the material interiority of the poem to metaphysical dualisms.

3. Osip Mandelstam opens up a dialogue with Dante about Hell, which is also a declaration regarding the path that the poem must take if it wants to be capable of pronouncing the "senseless name" of a time split in two by history and from then on disoriented.

4. Pier Paolo Pasolini rejects the category of history as a political category and proposes a new figure of political subjectivity that he names "pure light" or "the consciousness of the sun."

---

1. English in the original text. [TN]

16

5. In China, in the 1980s, the "Menglong" poets open up the question of what the poem can establish as a singular space of thought, when the poem takes the position of backing – without liquidating or straddling it – an enigmatic and obscure political sequence: namely the Cultural Revolution.

6. Gennadiy Aygi invents a poem "without particularities," in which each thing that exists, exists universally.

7. In his definitive poem – "The Broom" [*La Ginestra*] – Giacomo Leopardi is able to establish the figure of the Earth as a possible site of a human collective freed of any sort of transcendence, and who have, as their positive principle, the shared acceptance of contingency.

This list is obviously anything but comprehensive, it merely constitutes a small sampling of my circulation among poets and poems; many other examples are possible. My sole objective with this project is therefore to provide a bit of news from several poetic continents which are not identified or visited as much as they should be, and to incite readers to engage and develop these kinds of poetic readings. It is not a question of thinking "about" poems but *with poems*.

I. Stevens:
the illumination of seeming

For Wallace Stevens, the possibility of poetry itself rests upon the existence of an "interdependence between *imagination and reality as equals*." To put it another way: imagination and reality are the two edges of the capacity that Stevens attributes to the poem. And the poem is an archway going from one to the other: "Not only does imagination adhere to reality, but reality also adheres to imagination and their interdependence is essential."

Thus the poem does not merely remain on the side of imagination, with reality facing it. The poem is the site of interdependence between imagination and reality. More specifically: it is the singular site where they effectuate each other. If the poem was on one side, it would swing over to the side of reality and not that of imagination. Because "poetry and reality are one and the same thing, or should be. It is perhaps, adds the poet, less a thesis than a hypothesis." That which puts him to work, which moves him as a poet.

How does Stevens determine such a hypothesis? For him, reality is "things as they are [...], it is in and of itself, a jungle, each thing that it is composed of is a lone color. *So, first of all, there is reality*, which is held to be certain, latent, and which for the most part, is ignored." This threefold mode of the existence of reality contains a tension within it: held to be certain, it is actually latent, and ignored. Would the task of the poet then be to assure that it is, to render reality manifest, to produce a knowledge of it? The specific activity of the poem is none of these. While being somewhat provocative, Steven's provocation is that the poem is constructed in such a way as to ensure that reality *adheres* to imagination. The poem therefore strongly intervenes in the construction of reality.

But what is: "Imagination?" What is: "Reality?" In the work of Wallace Stevens, "imagination" must be distinguished from "fantasy." "Imagination" is not "fancy."[1] Stevens is loyal to the distinction established by Coleridge, loyal to what he considers as the "good Romanticism," that which grants the imagination its entire range of importance: "as far as the approach to truth is concerned, or say, to being by way of the imagination, Coleridge is one of the great figures." This is why Stevens sometimes wonders if the result, salvation, is not to be found on the side of Romanticism, even if he oftentimes diagnoses a poor use of imagination in its works: "Imagination is one of the greatest human powers. Romanticism belittles it. Imagination is the freedom of thought. Romanticism fails in making good use of this freedom. [...] Romanticism is the failure of imagination; in the same way sentimentality is the failure of feeling. Imagination is unique genius. It is intrepid and enthusiastic, and it is within abstraction that it finds its greatest achievement." The famous poem, "The Idea of Order at Key West," by way of a feminine form walking alongside the ocean singing, sketches an acute portrait of the singular power of imagination:

It was her voice that made
The sky acutest at its vanishing.
She measured to the hour its solitude.
She was the single artificer of the world
In which she sang. And when she sang, the sea,
Whatever self it had, became the self
That was her song, for she was the maker. Then we,
As we beheld her striding there alone,
Knew that there never was a world for her
Except the one she sang and, singing, made.

It is useful to add – in order to fully represent what Stevens intends by "imagination" – that he believes to have encountered, at the edges of the 1940s the measure of his most "decisive range of scope" not within poetry, literature, or art, but within international politics, and more specifically within the politics of

---

1. English in the original text. [TN]

communism. It is not a coincidence when, in 1936, Stevens begins the poem, "Owl's Clover," from the interior of the situation created by the Great Depression, with an immense meditation on the different modes of existence of the contemporary State – Western democratic States, socialist States, colonial States ... – and the necessity to question and distance oneself from them. And it is also not a coincidence that Lenin – next to Nietzsche – occupies a central place in the poem, "Description without Place":

Lenin, on a bench beside the lake disturbed
Swans. He was not a man for swans.

The slouch of his body and his look were not
In suavest keeping. The shoes, the clothes, the hat
Suited with decadence of those silences,
In which he sat. All chariots were drowned. The swans

Moved on the buried water where they lay.
Lenin took bread from his pocket, scattered it –

The swans fled outward to remoter reaches,
As if they knew of distant beaches; and were

Dissolved. The distances of space and time
Were one and swans far off were swans to come.

The eye of Lenin kept the far-off shapes.
His mind raised up, down-drowned, the chariots.

And reaches, beaches, tomorrow's regions became
One thinking of apocalyptic regions.

Here we find Lenin as a powerful figure of imagination, capable of fusing time and space with his thought, of conserving and bailing out a disappeared world in order to form with it, a new world, still to come. In order for reality to "adhere" to imagination, it still must of course be the real that imagination works on. Like a revolutionary leader, the poet must be aware that "one of the peculiarities of the imagination" is "always being at the end of an era": "[...] Imagination is always in the middle of attaching and adhering itself to a new reality. Not that there is a new imagination, but that there is a new reality." Images of imagination lose their strength as soon as they let themselves become distanced from reality. And when reality deserts the image, the poetic figure loses all vitality. The weakening of the image is always due to the "pressure of reality" which, in modifying itself, ruptures the unity of reality/imagination that alone grants the image the power of a real.

This reciprocal interaction of imagination/real is even more crucial in order for Stevens to characterize the 20th century as a time in which "the quest for supreme truth turns into the quest for an acceptable supreme fiction." From then on, truth and fiction have changed places, without in the least bit coinciding with skepticism: "the ultimate belief is to believe in a fiction that we know to be a fiction since there is nothing else but fictions. Absolute truth is knowing that it is a fiction and that we voluntarily believe in it." ("Adagia"). There is an upholding of the absoluteness of truth and at the same time a refusal of continuing to gauge truths via a supreme truth or some sort of transcendence. The poet's fate is not to make consolations regarding this state of things. On the contrary, the poet must share all "the confusions of intelligence" to which this situation exposes us, in order to be capable of extracting from them "the supreme fictions without which we are incapable of forming an idea [of the real]." From then on, the absolute is that of a fiction thought as fiction, but as a *supreme* fiction. The poems of Heaven and Hell have been written, Stevens declares, the task for us now is to write the "great poem of the earth."

These poems of the earth are destined to widen our thinking and ideas of the world. Stevens consecrated "Notes Toward a Supreme Fiction" to examine what the major characteristics of such fictions would be. They must contain, in this order, a capacity of abstraction, ("It Must Be Abstract"), a capacity to transform itself in view of change ("It Must Change"), and finally, it must have the capacity of giving pleasure ("It Must Give Pleasure").

Among the conditions that must be unified in order for such poems to emerge, must we include the existence of the poet himself? I think so. Stevens – who lives the life of an insurance agent, in the same way Pessoa lives the life of an office worker – clearly states: "The poet resembles everyone." "[…] I do not have at my disposal distinct modes of thinking for office work and poetic writing. I accomplish each task with the entirety of my spirit."

Previously, the poem didn't have to preoccupy itself with forging such supreme fictions: it could content itself on "repeating what was already in the script" ("Of Modern Poetry"). Why this word "repeating," and what would be repeated? The fundamental "script," that which defined the worldview, was the one written by the philosopher; it was the worldview of the philosopher. The poet was content on borrowing it from the philosopher without constituting poetry as its own specific ontological thinking, conscious of its singularity.

Stevens proceeds differently: he decides to consider (not without humor) philosophical truth as the "official conception of being," to which he opposes poetry as the "unofficial conception of being." In so doing, he declares himself completely aware of "granting poetry a much larger definition than we ordinarily grant it." Stevens strives to *contrast* poetry with philosophy at the same time that he strives to establish a *relation* between both of them. In truth, we are dealing with a new and singular gesture, that of placing philosophy and poetry into a "vis-à-vis" concerning an essential question: the thinking of being. Instituting a decisive relation between them and opening up the possibility of an intrinsic poetic ontology, distinct from the ontologies produced by metaphysics.

Bringing to an end – on the side of the poem – a long sequence initiated by the Platonic exclusion of the poets, Stevens postulates an *equality* between poetry and philosophy: "We must at least conceive poetry as being an equal to philosophy." Due to the fact that both of them share being neither on the side of opinion nor that of the organization of beliefs, Stevens sometimes even includes poetry in the space of philosophy: "Poetry can be seen as a phase of metaphysics," he writes. Nevertheless, Stevens never conceives poetry as capable of being confused with philosophy. For him, it is not a question of producing a "philosophical poetry" – no more than it is a question of conceiving a poetic philosophy. His counsel to the "The Figure of Youth as Virile Poet" is quite to the contrary, namely, to constantly be on guard against the speech and thought of the "swarm of character doubles [which are none other than] poetic philosophers and philosophical poets." Poetry cannot be double. The separation, the tension between poetry and philosophy are essential; they could only fuse together by losing themselves, the one as much as the other.

The "official" and "unofficial" concept of the image of being: is truly difficult. To the side of philosophy, it firmly distributes authority, power, and legality. But all evidence suggests that the image strives to tilt its preference toward the poem by insinuating the official concept cannot be the last word as far as being is concerned. Taking it back up, in order to turn it in the favor of poetry once again, and thus reversing Plato's verdict, Stevens maintains that poetry occupies a site which is completely foreign to the philosopher – this site being constituted by the perception of being "perfectly attuned with the idea that touches and the bird that sings." The ontological capacity of the poem can proceed from such a type of harmony, because reality is not capable of being thought as a fixed ensemble or as the image of a solid material:

> It is not in the premise that reality
> Is a solid. It may be a shade that traverses
> A dust, a force that traverses a shade
> ("An Ordinary Evening in New Haven, XXXI")

The poem must absolutely establish a proper ontological path; it must, as the short and dense poetic treatise "On Modern Poetry" suggests, "construct a new stage." The actor who steps onto this stage (the poet) is described as a "metaphysician in the dark" – with all the vagueness of this "dark." Thus this stage to be constructed remains arranged, within the interior of the poem, as a stage for metaphysics. But what is played out on this stage is the possibility of a new metaphysics: a metaphysics which is explicitly non philosophical.

In an essay, "Effects of Analogy," Stevens has this striking formula: "poetry is, at a degree of difficulty that is hard to believe, one of the effects of analogy." For Stevens, analogy is thus not a method or process of the poem. But on the contrary, the poem is viewed as resulting from the existence of analogy. This goes back to the conviction that the poem itself must produce what Stevens calls *a transcendental analog" of being*. He gives the poem, in the manner in which he pursues the project, a definition that is as magnificent as it is precise: "A poem is a detail of life which we have thought about for so long that thought becomes attached to it, becoming an inseparable part of it, or it is a detail of life felt with so much intensity that the sensation has penetrated it." We understand that a poem produces and organizes certain kinds of "crystallizations" of the imagination and the real, or better still, "this undefined number of *real things* that cannot be distinguished from *objects of the imagination.*"

Despite being "in the dark," the poet/actor is revealed to be capable of playing his instrument in such a manner that "sounds [pass] through sudden rightnesses, wholly / Containing the mind, below which it cannot descend, / Beyond which it has no will to rise." Thus, there exists a moment in the poem when it knows that it has arrived to the point of its own act of thinking, the point of the exact accuracy of what it thinks – at least if it struggles to be the poem of *the act of the mind.*[1]

Stevens strives to elucidate what the operations of thought are for such a poem. Such is the case in "Man Carrying Thing." This poem – whose title evokes that of a painting – is organized around two figures exempt from any clear identification: the vision of a "brune figure in winter evening" and that of a figure that is just as blurry as "the thing that he carries." In the presences of these two indistinct forms, the primary decision of the poem must be "to resist intelligence / Almost successfully." In other words, one must first of all fully accept that the brune figure will not let itself be identified – "*resists identity*" – and that the thing that it carries evades all signification, even the poorest one – "*resists / The most necessitous sense.*" The method of the poem will be to grasp these enigmatic figures as "secondary." Why qualify them as secondary? In order for the poem to treat them as parts of a whole ("*the obvious whole*") that are still poorly perceived, and whose existence it will not renounce posing the irrefutable evidence of.

Everything that the poem does not yet know what to name, must be considered as "uncertain particles" of a solid that is absolutely certain and which, from the beginning, is exempt from doubt – "*uncertain particles / Of the certain solid, the primary free from doubt.*" There can be no doubt as far as the real is concerned. When the world resists any identification, it's the fault of

---

1. English in the original text. [TN]

imagination and not that of the real. One cannot arrive at the true without confronting chaos and confusion. The poetic capture of the real requires exposing oneself to this turbulence of secondary things – the poem must know how to endure *"the storm of secondary things."* Because the real does not let itself be easily distinguishable from the non real. All things that are not yet known first present themselves as unreal as the real can be. The poem has to accept being the prey of vague, fluid, floating things, like the snowflakes of a dreadful mental storm, which it must overcome in order to arrive at the *"bright obvious"* of the true:

> We must endure our thoughts all night, until
> The bright obvious stands motionless in the cold.

"A difficulty that we affirm," declares "An Ordinary Evening in New Haven" – XIII, it is "the difficulty of the visible / To the nations of the clear invisible." This partition between the visible and invisible is at once directly taken from Plato and yet also transformed by Stevens. In Plato, the myth of the cave presents a situation of original separation between the being exposed to the visible and the being exposed to thought. For those chained in the cave, the first site of the visible is a site devoted to shadows, even to the shadows of shadows, and thus to the semblant. For the one pulled out of the cave and thrown into the great light, the sun certainly provides the gift of a new visible, which the gaze accustomed to the shadows has a hard time being able to support in the beginning. But to conclude that the true is on the side of the visible revealed by the sun supposes one more step: to conceive via difference, that the visible world of the cave is false. And yet this one extra step does not come from the lone visible, or from the lone sun, it comes from the exposure of the visible to thought. And thus from this separate site of the visible and the sensible that Plato calls the intelligible or the thinkable. As for Stevens, he characterizes the to and fro of the poem between the world and the word as a constant to and fro between an "uncertain visible" and a "clear invisible." On one hand, the referent remains the visible. But on the other hand, Stevens accentuates the fact that, within the poem, the visible is always captive to the invisible, to the extent that everything is composed of words. This point is essential: verbal resemblances, for example, are from then on, abstract and not sensible. The thought specific to the poem is formed within the singular endurance with which it conjugates the uncertainty of the visible and the illuminating production of an *invisible* that does not belong to the Platonic site of the *intelligible*.

Stevens closely examines metaphor, which plays a crucial role for him within the properly poetic articulation of a visible and an invisible. Staying within the pages of "Effects of Analogy," Stevens defines the use he makes of it: metaphor "connects, it is the basis for *appearance*." For him, metaphor – which moreover, he prefers to give the name "metamorphosis" – does not enunciate an identity; it constructs a resemblance. One should not equate resemblance with imitation – which Stevens describes as a "failed identity" between two things. Resemblance "completes and reinforces what two different things have in common. It makes them shine." This is why "the proliferation of resemblances enlarges an object." As the poem that also has the title of a painting ("Study of Two Pears") subtly expresses, the network of resemblances – far from providing a way of seeing and thinking that a thing would be "the same" as another – shows to what extent this thing only resembles itself:

> The pears are not viols,
> Nudes or bottles.
> They resemble nothing else.

"Viols," "nudes," "bottles," are here compared to "pears," in order to better see what these latter are/aren't: neither viols, nor nudes, nor bottles. Whereas what they are is "enlarged" by these resemblances.

This use of metaphor is at the service of an ontological prescription: The poet

> [...] must say nothing of the fruit that is
> Not true, nor think it, less. He must defy
> The metaphor that murders metaphor.
> He seeks as image a second of the self,
> ("Someone Puts a Pineapple Together," *Three Academic Pieces*)

Whatever distinction we grant the verb "defy" in this central utterance: "*He must defy / The metaphor that murders metaphor*," one thing is certain: for Stevens, there is metaphor and metaphor. And only a metaphor that allows for the possibility of "a second of the self" should be the object of the poet's attention. Must one also understand the image of the poem as "a second" of the self? That it occurs to help the self in that it composes appearance in words?

When Stevens accentuates the fact that "the words of a poet speak of things that do not exist without *words*," this is what he is getting at: figures of poetic language cannot be rhetorical figures, they must be figures "that participate" with the being of things itself. The metaphor that is susceptible to speaking the truth of fruit is not an affair of subjective vision. The production of such a vision has as its stakes to bring to the light of day what Stevens does not hesitate calling the "participants of its being":

"We awake, [...]
Inside the interior itself of the object we are looking for,
Which participates with its being.
("Study of Images I")

To make further progress concerning this difficult question of a properly poetic ontology requires us to enter into the detail of a poem that I take as essential: "Description without place." Its first line contains a decisive utterance:

It is possible that to seem – is to be.

We must think how an equivalence of "to seem/to be" is possible under certain conditions – which, as the poem will demonstrate, are those of poetic conditions. We should immediately state that there is a major difficulty in translating the semantic apparatus in which "to seem" is inscribed in French. This difficulty rests upon a considerable questioning of what Stevens is aiming at with "to seem." In this respect, it is a key point that from now on, the equivalence of "to seem/to be" is posited not as a given, but as *possible*. Indeed, if we see an emphasis placed on the pure and simple existence of equivalence, we would be within one of the components of a sophistic thesis concerning the indiscernibility of appearances and beings, of "to seem" and "to be." And yet, in the work of Stevens, we are not dealing with an utterance of sophistry concerning being, but on the contrary, we are dealing with a major thesis concerning the capacity of poetic ontological thought for inscribing "to be" within "to seem." To put it provisionally: *un être dans un apparaître*. A being within a seeming.

In English, "to seem" and "seeming" are of the semantic register of "to resemble," "resemblance," and obviously not of the register of "to appear," "appearance," "apparition." In the French language however, the existence of the double *sembler/paraître* as well as the terms *"le semblant," "la semblance," "le paraître,"* opens up a possible derivation toward the semantic field of appearance. Which, moreover, is how Bernard Noël chose to translate the essence of "to seem" as *paraître*, "to appear," and "seeming" as *apparence*. But if his choice is on the side of appearance, on the one hand we see that the part of the semantic field linked to the idea of resemblance is lost; and on the other hand, we see the differences between "seeming" and the terms "apparition" and "appearance" are reduced, even though these words emerge later on with force in the poem.

For me, it seems, that the difficulty resides in grasping the following: via the couple "to seem" / "to be." For Stevens, it is indeed a question of thinking the properly poetic entanglement of appearing and being. What matters for him is demonstrating that in his own language – by way of the network of *resemblances*, the poem organizes – appearance, and that far from being a faux semblant, composes a being with it. And that, within the poem, there can exist something like an *"appar-être,"* "seeming." And this is how I propose to translate "seeming."

This word from the poet cannot be reduced to the philosophical category of the semblant (which opens up the sophistic hypothesis of the being as pure simulacra), or to that of appearance (which would call forth the Platonic doublet of appearance and essence – that is completely rejected by Stevens).

Indeed, Stevens' investigation is not attempting to oppose being and appearance but rather to dissolve their separation. His investigation bears – and this is its great point of proximity to the thought of Caeiro – on the possibility of what we could call an "absolute" poetic thought. Which is to say, a thought, which, in its composition of singular *seemings*, is even up to the task of grasping the being "without remainder." Or to put it in Stevens' words, a thought which truly deploys itself as "part of the res itself, and not about it" ("An Ordinary Evening in New Haven – XII").

Poetry – at least when it attempts to make itself a "description without place" – is revealed to even be capable of grasping being in the form of seeming.

"Description without place" is one of the possible names for the poem. Each poem organizes a singular type of "description." But the poem itself is "without place," its descriptions are without place because there is nothing that exists as a general site, or as a general "doctrine," of being. Nor is there anything of the being in the world that is positioned toward a primary interiority, or toward a certain awareness of it. It is the real that is primary. There is world even before we exist in this world. And this world is pure exteriority. "Notes Toward a Supreme Fiction" – 1.4 is insistent concerning this point:

> The clouds preceded us.
>
> There was a muddy center before we breathed. [...]
>
> From this the poem springs: that we live in a place
> That is not our own and, much more, not ourselves
> And hard it is in spite of blazoned days.
>
> We are the mimics. Clouds are pedagogues.

The same idea is taken back up, in "Anecdote of Men by the Thousand," regarding the soul (the figure par excellence of interiority) which one must posit is made by that which is external to it:

> The soul, he said, is composed
> Of the external world

One should also pay attention to the word "compose," because this word opens up the entanglement, by way of and within the poem, of a "there is" (at once appearance and being) and of a being. The descriptions of the poems have as a particularity that they only say being by way of and within its places. This is uttered from the very beginning of the first strophe of the poem:

There are men of the East, he said,
Who are the East.
There are men of a province
Who are that province.
There are men of a valley
Who are that valley.

Still more important is the final strophe, because the articulation of the visible/invisible at the heart of what I propose calling the hypothesis of seeming, is described:

The dress of a woman of Lhassa,
In its place,
Is an invisible element of that place
Made visible.

The dress of a woman of Lhassa is an illustration of what Stevens will name, in one of his last poems, "*local objects.*" "*Local objects,*" which he will also say are "*the objects of insight,*" "*the integrations of feeling,*" and finally "*the things that came of their own accord.*" The existence of such objects is rare and is not a given. They are "*objects not present as a matter of course.*" Their existence depends on new names ("a fresh name") that will or will not be able to produce the poem. Naming the dress of a woman of Lhassa, the poem makes something emerge that belongs to the place (Lhassa), but which was an "invisible element." The dress, named by the poem, renders the place visible as place. Or better still: the latent being of the place ceases being invisible, the dress makes it seem [*appar-être*].

To put it another way, without the freshness of names that the poem composes, being – which is always localized – remains invisible. And yet, poetic language is not an "expression" of being, even less the general "place" of being. It makes place *seem* [*appar-être*] within the description of the poem, on the condition of knowing how to go:

[…] straight to the word,
Straight to the transfixing object, to the object
At the exactest point at which it is itself,
("An Ordinary Evening in New Haven"– IX)

31

The figure of the sun in "Description without place" – this sun which is placed there as "an example" – elucidates Stevens' ontological vision. This example is indeed singular and strong since the initial thesis of the poem ("It is possible that to seem – is to be") is literally founded upon the verse that follows: "As the sun is something seeming and it is." Because for the sun, we can say that "what it seems, it is," and we can also affirm this by the resemblance it has with all things:

Thus things are like a seeming of the sun.

Unlike in Plato, the sun does not have as its function to reveal that things were not as they appeared to be within the darkness of the cave. The sun incarnates the possibility of the grasping of being shielded from (in a poem that is not by chance titled, "The Latest Freed Man," ... from the Platonic cave) a "doctrine" of being. The sun is the description of a being without description:

It was how the sun came shining into his room:
To be without a description of to be [...]

In "Notes Toward a Supreme Fiction – I," Stevens completes this portrait:

There is a project for the sun. The sun
Must bear no name, gold flourisher, but be
In the difficulty of what it is to be.

The sun must not bear a name (even though the poem paradoxically gives it the name of gold flourisher) and this is because it must stand within "the difficulty of what it is to be." For Stevens however, "to be" has no general name. Nor can any general description of it exist. To be can only be expressed as an identified emerging multiplicity.

One should however pay the greatest attention to the affirmation in "An Ordinary Evening in New Haven, XXIII" according to which the sun *is* "half the world, half everything, / The bodiless half" of all things. This being that cannot be named composes half of what its light renders visible.

The problem is that in the poem where things appear as verses and words, they can retain their status of "dilapidate / appearances of what appearances," (I) unless the poem shows itself capable of inscribing "an escape from repetition, a happening / In *space and the self.*" (XXIV). For the poet, it is first of all given as something that is emerging and something that is changing within the visible. Seeming is an emergence. This is why Stevens' greatest ambition, even his obsession, is that the poem proves itself capable of always grasping that which changes within the real. The poem must be able to perceive what our attention typically has trouble grasping: The "less legible" meanings of sounds, the little reds / Not often realized, the lighter words / In the heavy drum of speech" (XXXI) or on a different register, a destitute and abandoned woman, rejected by the Great Depression, with which "Owl's Clover" opens. He has to know how to describe things as surprising as "[the] inner men / Behind the outer shields, the sheets of music / In the strokes of thunder, dead candles at the window / When day comes, fire-foams in the motion of the sea [...]" (An Ordinary Evening in New Haven, XXXI).

Above all, he must be capable of perceiving what is changing within the moment before this change becomes perceivable by everyone. Stevens hates monumental art that is in part linked with the massiveness of the State. On the contrary, Stevens wants to be an artist who, even within his longer poems, pays the subtlest attention to the possible as well as to change. Verse VI of "Mr Burnshaw and the Statue" in "Owl's Clover" wondrously describes the imperative and importance of such moments:

It is only enough
To live incessantly within change. See how
On a day still full of summer, when the leaves
Appear to sleep within a sleeping air,
They suddenly fall, and the leafless sound of the wind
Is no longer a sound of summer. So great a change
Is constant.

The poem must "defamiliarize" us with the supposed state of the world. The terms earth, heavens, tree, and clouds must rid themselves of the old usage that was attributed to them: the poem must dare to "throw away the lights, the definitions," and "say of what you see in the dark." Then, we will conceive that:

> The Earth, for us, is flat and bare.
> There are no shadows.

And that

> Poetry
> Exceeding music must take the place
> Of empty heaven and its hymns [...]

("The Man with the Blue Guitar," XXXII and V)

II. Caeiro:
a desire for a "metaphysics without metaphysics" within poems

Before becoming a poet – which for Fernando Pessoa, meant suddenly becoming four distinct poets he would later decide to call heteronyms – Pessoa had diagnosed an impossibility and a crisis: the crisis of metaphysics and the end of any consistent philosophical apparatus. From this he concludes the impossibility of any elaborate great poetry – any poetry worthy of this name, for Pessoa, would seem to require propping itself up by conceptions from a philosophy.

The emergence, on March 8, 1914, of a quartet of heteronymous poets – Caeiro, the Master, his two disciples, Reis and Campos, and the orthonym, Fernando-Pessoa-In-Person – completely upset the terms of how the problem had been posed. Not that what emerged presented itself to Pessoa in full clarity. On the contrary, he was the first who was capable of forcing himself to think and name what presented itself, as far as poetry is concerned: the poem had to cease being under the condition of philosophy and had to constitute a place where thinking the ontological incapacity of metaphysics after Kant could be thought and where one could elaborate a properly poetic ontology. The coincidence between Stevens' and Pessoa's projects is all the more striking in that they didn't know each other at all and the poetic means by which they invented such projects are completely dissimilar.

Within the inaugural multiplicity of the Pessoan poetic apparatus – the existence of a conjunction or a constellation of *four* poets – a primary invention becomes manifest: the possibility of identifying, from the interior of several distinct poetic sites, a number of questions inherited from the crisis of metaphysics that haunts Pessoa. What can a thought of being be once it is presented as a figure internal to the poem, born by the poem? What of the entangled questions of non-being, of nothing, and nothingness? What could the contents be of a wisdom that is in accordance with a vision of being, of humanity, and of the universe that does not refer to a signification or meaning? How do we prepare the poem for the challenge of inscribing infinity?

In the eyes of Pessoa, the emergence of the poet, Alberto Caeiro, and above all his work, *The Keeper of Sheep*, constitutes a decisive turn, a veritable caesura, not only within his own history as a poet, but within the entire history of poetry. The poems of the Keeper in effect inaugurate an ascetic practice of "seeing without thinking," which allows him to reunite with the Parmenidean conviction that "being and thinking are the same." Under this gaze, "clear as a sunflower," things are exactly as they appear to be and are not susceptible to interpretation. "The unique intimate signification of things, / is that they don't have any intimate signification."

However, the orthonymous poetic oeuvre of Fernando-Pessoa-in-Person (which proliferates within numerous poems from the *Cancioneiro*) claims that this vision of being as "things" does not deal with the question of the existence of non-being and so does not resolve it. Contrary to the solar poetry of the Keeper of Sheep, this second poet – who "inexists" when Caeiro writes – quietly objects. His infinitely subtle poems, slipping like water through fingers, strive to apprehend the unstable reversibility of being and non-being.

March 8, 1914, Ricardo Reis does not yet appear in poems, but within the figure of a poet with neoclassicist inspiration, nourished by Latin and Greek poetry. In reality, his specific place as a poet largely depends on the complete deployment of Caeiro's oeuvre: it will become the task of Reis to explore in what way the proposition of the *Keeper of Sheep* (to think being, man, and the universe under the unique name of "things") can open up the understanding that within the universe man has no meaning, no more meaning than all the "things" that compose it. Reis invents a positive wisdom, a strong and new subjectivity that rejects nihilism without conceding to a transcendence, and calmly returns to the gods their fictional being.

Alvaro de Campos is the last to emerge as a tormented disciple of the Master: his effervescent and melancholy oeuvre confronts Caeiro's innovations with poetic post-romantic conditions, with an urban and machinic universe (no longer the natural countryside found in Caeiro), and above all with the question of infinity, - a question which Caeiro's oeuvre deliberately ignores.

For more details regarding this multiple apparatus, I return to my book, *Pessoa, The Metaphysical Courier* [*Pessoa, le passeur métaphysique*, 2006 Seuil]. More specifically, I would like to focus on the first of the four heteronymous poets – Alberto Caeiro – who is the Master of the three others, because his oeuvre opens and supports a poetic frontal attack on metaphysics. Caeiro first of all identifies this metaphysics as being a characteristic found within poetry itself, when poetry attributes a hidden signification to things, when it places a meaning onto the universe, when it ties the existence of the world to first causes and final ends. Without questioning either one of them, poetry spontaneously works from the interior of dual categories, such as thought and being, subject and object, consciousness and world. And these dualities adhere to the poem, to its materiality, its language, by way of double meaning, symbol, and metaphor. This is why ridding oneself of the mode of metaphysical thinking is an operation that must be effectuated inside the poem, and requires a profound transformation of the being of the poem.

If Caeiro can be designated as the Master of the heteronymous poets, it is first of all because he strives to subtract the poem, within its own materiality, from the inherent and omnipresent grip of these metaphysical dualisms. The poem of the Keeper is written and thought of as a kind of re-education of a gaze that has become unable to "see without setting out to think," because for a long time it has been modeled on the categories of appearance and essence, subject and object, or consciousness and world. The innovation proposed by Caeiro is that of a poem of "non-thought" and of "seeing," in which a thought becomes possible that is no longer a "thinking" in a metaphysical sense. This thought has as its site, the gaze:

The main thing is knowing how to see,
To know how to see without thinking,
To know how to see when you see,
And not to think when you see
Or see when you think.

But this (poor us who dress up souls!)
This takes deep study,
An apprenticeship in unlearning. [...]
[Poem XXIV, *The Keeper of Sheep*]

The gaze that is capable of "only seeing the visible" can attain a true, and no longer deceptive, access to things. It is a gaze that rejects the Platonic split between (fallacious) appearance and (true) essence:

What we see of things is things.
Why would we see one thing if there is something else?
How could seeing and hearing be an illusion
If seeing and hearing are truly seeing and hearing?
[Poem XXIV]

One should immediately note that "things" is not an empirical designation for Caeiro: it is the name under which a "seeing," which is that of the poem, affirms its capacity of a grasping of being without remainder and without transcendence. And nevertheless, in the same way the philosopher must free man from the illusion of appearances and lead him to support the blinding sun of the Idea, the poet underlines that simply seeing things, in reality, requires "profound study," a singular apprenticeship of "unlearning."

For, in order to learn to see things as things, one must unlearn the way in which metaphysics models the gaze focused on them. This is affirmed in the first poem from "Disassembled Poems," which violently denounces philosophy's capacity to truly gain access to an outside:

It is not enough to open the window
in order to see the fields and the river.
It is not enough to not be blind
in order to see the trees and flowers.
One must also have no philosophy whatsoever.

With philosophy there are no trees: there are only ideas.
There is only each one of us, like a cave.
There is only a closed window, and the entire universe on the outside;
and the dream of what we could see if the window would open,
and which is never that which we see when the window opens [...]

Whereas Caeiro takes up the challenge of opening a window onto the universe in such a way that what we see is truly what we see, he does not hesitate discrediting those philosophers and poets that he considers to be "mystics":

Today I read nearly two pages
In a book by a mystic poet.
And I laughed like someone who'd been weeping and weeping.

Mystic poets are sick philosophers.
And philosophers are madmen. [...]

As for myself, I write the prose of my poems
And I am satisfied
Because I know all I can understand is Nature from the outside;
I don't understand it from inside.
Because Nature hasn't any inside;
It wouldn't be Nature otherwise.
[Poem XXVIII]

Here we have another remarkable utterance by Caeiro: "Nature hasn't any inside." To put it another way, things are pure exteriority. And we, in belonging to the world of things, "before being inside we are outside / and so, we are essentially external." The Keeper of Sheep – a fictitious figure whose name graces the title of Caeiro's book – a solitary character, either walking in the sun, or rain, accompanying his sheep, and always thinking, mumbling, and talking, like shepherds who have lived alone for a long time are accustomed to doing. The recovery of this figure, from the bucolic tradition, functions as a global metaphorical framework, allowing us to demand from each poem the imperative and practice of producing a new gaze, but also allows us to then subtract the quasi-totality of poetic material under the influence of metaphor. Having barely been sketched, this figure is then erased and shown to be fictitious: "I never kept sheep, but it's as if I've done so." The sheep of the Keeper are merely his thoughts, thoughts he gazes upon from the outside in the same way he would gaze upon his animals.

Clarity, precision, lucidity, an almost quasi-tautological translucence characterize most of the poems in *The Keeper of Sheep*. These qualities are the result of the production of a language that passes beyond the privacy of writing and grants a voice to each poem that, above all else, speaks to itself, that speaks out loud with all the immediacy and flexibility and the possibilities of repetition and hesitation a voice has at its disposal. The poem of the Keeper pronounces thought more than it writes thought. Each poem inscribes within itself the precarity of speech, accepting the risk of a specific awkwardness, allowing for repetitions. This projection of thought into voices allows us to compare the emergence of the poem with the emergence of things for the gaze.

This is exactly what poem XLVI from *The Keeper of Sheep* attempts to take into account:

In one way or another,
The moment permitting,
Able to say what I think at times,
And otherwise saying it poorly or jumbled,
I keep writing my poems without wanting to,
As if writing weren't something made up of gestures,
As if writing were something that happened to me
Like the sun outside shining on me.

But Caeiro equally leans on the exteriority of his speech in order to grasp, by the power of voice, thought outside of any interiority to itself. As an example, amid many others, I will provide this excerpt of poem XXXIX from *The Keeper of Sheep*:

The mystery of things, where is it?
Where is that which never appears
to show us, at least, it's a mystery?
What's the river know about it and what, the tree?
And I, being no more than they, what do I know about it?
Whenever I look at things and think what men think of them,
I laugh like a brook freshly sounding off a rock.

Because the only hidden meaning of things
Is that they have no hidden meaning at all
This is stranger than all the strangenesses,
And the dreams of all the poets,
And the thoughts of all the philosophers –
That things really are what they appear to be
And that there is nothing to understand.

Yes, here's what my senses have learned all by themselves:
Things have no meaning – they have existence.
Things are the only hidden meaning of things.

This soliloquy from the shepherd is a constant quarrel with questions from metaphysics that have entered into the heart of the poem itself: here, the evocation of the "mystery" of things, of the hypothesis that they have a "hidden meaning," opens up a line of questioning concerning figures of transcendence. To keep these sorts of questions at a distance, the poet thinks of himself as being no more than a tree or a river. He makes himself a thing among things: "I laugh like a brook freshly sounding off a rock," he writes before peacefully uttering that things "are really what they appear to be," and radically withdrawing from any meaning or signification: they don't have meaning, they have existence.

It so happens that this intertwining of voices exiles the poem to the edge of the poetic and non-poetic, pushing it in a way to the limits of prose. This is what those who do not like this poet object to – that what he writes is not "poetry." But this inclination of the poem toward prose is entirely directed by the thought of the Keeper who, moving away from metaphysics, must also break with a certain regime of poetry, that he defines as artistic poetry or as poetry thought of as an art. For the Keeper, separating poetry from art means withdrawing the poem from any formal external order (rhymes, rhythm, prosody, tropes ...). And this is what he installs within the vicinity of prose, whose existence, contrary to the poem, is *a priori* formless.

It is true that the Keeper's poetry strives to create an *artless* regime of the poetic. For it is the art of the poets that Caeiro accuses of introducing ulterior motives and metaphysical double meanings into the poem. Art is the exigency of forms, and by this alone, is the instance, par excellence, of the subjective.

However, Caeiro is not so much striving to produce an "objective" poetry – as Reis sometimes claims – but to completely destroy any distinction of subject/object. To do this, he must separate the poem from all poetic art in placing it under the sole constraint that he is striving to produce – that is, a thinking that is a "seeing without thinking." To work on one's poems like a carpenter works his planks, to place a line upon another line as if constructing a wall, is precisely what Caeiro cannot and will not do. Contrary to the artist poets, he proposes the image of a poem as pure flourishing. It is a question of letting the thought of the poem perform, as much as it can, a separation within the prose. Poem XXXV from *The Keeper of Sheep* is worth contemplating in that it focuses within the texture itself of this opposition between the art of the poets and what Caeiro rightly calls, in Poem XXVIII, "the prose of my lines":

The moonlight behind the tall branches
The poets all say is more
Than the moonlight behind tall branches.

But for me, who does not know what I think,
What the moonlight behind the tall branches
Is, beyond its being
The moonlight behind the tall branches,
Is not being more
Than the moonlight behind the tall branches.

This poem also demonstrates – and this is where its value resides, in its simplicity – how Caeiro's will is to maintain the poetic capacity to think being. It is indeed a question of saying what the moonlight "is" (contrary to what "the poets all say is more"). But to establish an ontological capacity in the poem (that philosophy has lost) supposes inventing an entirely new regime of poetics.

Against all Romanticism, the Keeper pronounces the inexistence of "Nature" as a signifying set. Poem XLVII strongly declares:

I saw that there was no Nature,
That Nature does not exist,
That there are mountains, valleys, plains,
That there are trees, flowers, grasses,
That there are rivers and stones,

But that there is not one great All these things belong to,
That any really authentic unity
Is a sickness of all our ideas.

Nature is simply parts, nothing whole.

But the Keeper also presents himself in Poem XLVI as the "unique poet of Nature," the veritable "Discoverer" of the universe in so far as he states in a specifically new way its non signifying truth:

I'm the Argonaut of true sensations.
I bring a new Universe into the Universe
Because I bring to the Universe its very own self.

It would be hard to find a more magnificent way to declare an absolute confidence in the ontological capacities of the poem.

Ultimately, what is performed within the Keeper's oeuvre is more than simply a total rejection of metaphysics; it is the desire to stave off any singular metaphysical configuration: the various dualistic splitting of thought and being, circulating from philosophy to the poem, and preventing the poem to grasp things as things. Hence the decision to substitute for the different metaphysical modes of thinking a "seeing without thinking," and the extreme singularity of the Keeper's oeuvre where what we could call a *poetic distancing of metaphysics* is effectuated.

Regarding this point, it is possible to consider Caeiro's oeuvre as a striking first attempt at breaking – from the interior of the poem – with what Quentin Meillasoux, in his beautiful book, *After Finitude,* identifies, from the interior of philosophy, as the unchallenged domination of correlationism. For it is certain that Caeiro-thought partly revives the figure of the Universe as absolute Outside: an outside that is pure exteriority, un-correlated to any thought and any human existence. Here one should largely cite the Disassembled poem that contains so many surprising utterances:

- Being real means not being inside myself.
I have no notion of reality inside my person.

- [...] my soul can only be defined in terms of the outside.

43

- If the soul is more real
Than the exterior world, as you say, philosopher
Why was the exterior world given to me as the model of reality?

On the other hand, the Keeper affirms that it is possible to think this radical exteriority, once "to think" is replaced by "do not think" in which the exteriority of the Universe to the self is given as wrapped up within the inevitable interiority of the self of thought. One must hold on to this ideal of a "not thinking" which is traced upon the exteriority of the Universe to self:

I think and write like flowers have color.
But with less perfection in my way of expressing myself.
Because I lack the divine simplicity
Of wholly being *only my exterior.*
[Poem XIV]

I am the size of what I see,
Not the size of my height....
[Poem VII]

Without thinking, I have the Earth and the Sky.
[Poem XXXIV]

Whatever we end up doing, "there is enough metaphysics in not thinking," Poem V remarks and protests. Caeiro does not pronounce so much the complete destruction of metaphysics as he strives to poetically establish what we could call a "metaphysics without metaphysics." Whereas Meillasoux announces that the problems with metaphysics are true even if they should be reformulated from within the interior of an affirmation of contingency as absolute point, Caeiro takes back up, one after the other, the interrogations of metaphysics, so as not to exactly posit against them the end of metaphysics but, a "better" metaphysics, the metaphysics of trees and grass which live without knowing why they live. In which they are closer and more consistent with the immanent senseless truth of the Universe:

Metaphysics? What metaphysics do those trees have?
Of being green and bushy and having branches
And of giving fruit in their own time, which doesn't make us think,
To us who don't know how to pay attention to them.
But what better metaphysics than theirs,
Which is not knowing what they live for
Not even knowing that they don't know?
[Poem V]

Each poem must become the practice field for a new type of seeing, capable of grasping being as "things" and to thus bear a vision
of humanity and the universe removed from any transcendence.
These two aspects of Caeiro-thought are concentrated within an
unforgettable formula from one of the "Disassembled poems":
"To be a thing is to not be susceptible to interpretation."

In so doing, it becomes a question of *keeping*, within the poem,
the ontological ambition which philosophy after Kant gave up
on: so it is that the strange name of the "Keeper" that the abstract
shepherd bears is elucidated, for Caeiro, as the figure of a new
poet. The poems of the Keeper invent a new ontological site from
where the poet can affirm with serene contentment that inhabits
him (in "Disassembled Poems"):

The terrifying reality of things
is my discovery everyday.
Each thing is what it is,
and it is hard to explain how much this makes me happy
and how much it is enough.
To exist is enough to be complete.

III. What does Mandelstam Discuss with Dante?

Mandelstam describes the intellectual crisis in which he finds himself as such: on the one hand,

> The dimness, the unstructured nature of nineteenth century European scientific thought, by the time of the turn of the present century, had completely demoralized scientific thought. Intellect, which does not consist of a mere aggregate of knowledge, but rather of "grasping," technique, and method, abandoned science since intellect can exist independently and can find its own nourishment where convenient. Searching for intellect in precisely this sense in European scientific life would be futile. The free intellect of man had removed itself from science. It turned up everywhere, but not there: in poetry, in mysticism, in politics, in theology ("About the Nature of the Word").

and on the other hand,

> All the sciences were turned into their own abstract and monstrous methodologies (with the exception of mathematics). [...] Most typical was philosophy: through the whole stretch of the century it preferred to limit itself to "Introductions to Philosophy," kept introducing without end, led you out somewhere or other, and then abandoned it ("The 19th Century").

From this flows science's damaging distaste for the poem as well as a contempt for philosophy, which according to Mandelstam can only regain its footing by taking the mindset of rigor and knowledge as well as the will of truth. I would like to attempt to show here how this will had become consolidated and confirmed from within what the Russian poet himself designated as his "conversation" with Dante (a book he wrote between 1930-1933 in the hell of Crimea/Taurida which was victim to the famine unleashed by the anti-kulak struggle) but also how this encounter allowed him to think his own time as essentially disoriented and the consequences drawn from this disorientation.

The nature of time in Dante is most certainly what first touches Mandelstam: "[...] Dante altered the structure of time, or perhaps, the other way around: he was forced to resort to a glossolalia of facts, to a synchronism of events, names, and traditions separated by centuries, precisely because he heard the overtones of time." He states with acuity. "The method chosen by Dante is one of anachronism [...]."

Mandelstam himself claims that it is by way of Einstein's illuminations that he understands the temporal manipulations of Dante: "Thanks to such change in our time, the conception of the unity of time has been shaken, and it is no accident that contemporary mathematical science has advanced the principle of relativity" ("About the Nature of the Word"). Relativity allows him to think the density of historical events, to think them in terms other than cause and effect, and to examine their capacity to break with a linear and oriented flow of time.

This is necessary when he meditates on his own century whose spine was "broken" under the weight of the Bolshevik revolution, within a new era, where it was a question of arriving at uttering "the senseless name." Mandelstam conceives as one of his tasks to form the name of this event, unprecedented in history, and whose political nomination as revolution is not enough.

Even before the October Revolution of 1917, in a striking poem from 1915, in the middle of World War I (a poem where he likens Russia to the figure he names "Phaedra-night"), Mandelstam already shows that his task as a poet will be "by our dirge / escorting the dead," to "tame the black sun that rises / that raged and would not sleep / that is suddenly smoldering in the country – like that of Phaedra in Troezen."

In a poem that comes from November 1917, just after the events of October, the poet feels destined to wear "a black miter," gathering up "a blind world, racked with argument":

Who knows, maybe my candle won't last,
and right in broad daylight I'll drop into night [...]
wear a black miter on my head:
Like the dilatory patriarch, in ruined Moscow,
unconsecrated world on my head,
racked with argument, blind, blind,

Then again, in a poem from 1920, "Heaviness and Tenderness"

I have one purpose left in the world, a golden purpose,
how to exhaust the burden of time, its fever.

To put it another way: when the people's leader must bear, "with tears," "the dark *burden of power*" (as Mandelstam describes in 1918 poem: "Brothers, Let Us Celebrate the Twilight of Liberty...."), the eminent purpose of the poet, his "golden purpose" becomes that of "*exhausting the burden of time.*"

Alain Badiou and Jacques Rancière among others, have analyzed several of the operations by which Mandelstam's poems induce a mode of being present to the present that opens large historico-political questions about the time in which he strives to live. They have commented on his great poems: "The Century," "Finder of a Horseshoe," and "The Twilight of Freedom." They show how Mandelstam installs thought within a fundamental historical disorientation: after October 1917, thinking time is to think the century as split into two sections that are from then on separate, thus it is a way of thinking time starting from ruptures and not within an oriented history of continuity, to refuse any principle of generating the present by way of the past, any genealogical thought, in terms of cause and effect.

They also show how for Mandelstam, the poem can no longer be the breath of nature or History. Because the air has become unbreathable, saturated as it is by words, comparisons, metaphors, the language of politics and the State, that set out for the conquest of time in order to cover it back up, which thus renders time unthinkable and indecipherable. And how Mandelstam's critique of Symbolism not only takes aim at a certain practice and philosophy of language, but simultaneously a philosophy of history and a practice of politics. It is vital for Mandelstam that a free play between words and things remains open, because naming must fully be in play as a principle of truth at a moment where the new State has a voracious need for words, in order to paste images of the new life onto its body.

Here I would like to cite Mandelstam himself: "To show compassion for the State which denies the word is the contemporary poet's civic "way," the heroic feat that awaits him" ("The Word and Culture"). It is around the word that a singular fate is developed between the poet and the State, under the strange banner and tonality of the poet's "compassion" for the State. What does "the State which denies the word" mean coming from the mouth of Mandelstam? The use of the word that the State makes is a usage that denies itself of the word. Which is to say, the manner in which the word floats around things, without ever being irrevocably attached to them, but also the way in which the word must be capable of freely choosing the thing – and if this isn't the case, we fail and enter into an artificial and fallacious world, deprived of all truth.

The "social purpose" of the "contemporary poet," in contrast to the State that is famished for words, is to ensure the event of the random encounter of words and things. The poem must be the site where words and things recognize themselves, but just as quickly separate, in order to identify with each other anew.

For Mandelstam, and in this way he is close to Dante, to think that the present does not linearly come out of the past demands thinking in what manner the past can return within the present, beyond the event caesura. The poem must make itself into a "poem-plow": it must know how to turn the rich soil of time, to rip away from it the words and names that the illusion of the continuity of historical time places behind us, and which, on the contrary we can fully bring back among us, recovering the rising force that is attached to them. As Jacques Rancière rightly remarks concerning Mandelstam, Greece for example, is not a place outside the poem, it is completely inside the poem that he cites.

In this way Neva and Lethe are "transparent to each other" like Cassandra and Troy are on October 1917, but also like Dante and Florence – in this poem written in exile on March 16, 1937 on the hills of the Voronezh:

> No comparisons: Everyone alive is incomparable.
> With sweet fright
> I'd agree with the steppe's smooth equality, and
> The sky's circle was like a sickness.

> I'd turn to the servant-air
> waiting for news, for something,
> and get ready to leave, and I'd drift down an arc
> of journeys that never begin.

> Wherever I've got more sky – I'll wander there, yes –
> but this bright boredom won't let me leave
> these young Voronezh hills, won't let me go
> to those universal hills – there, clear, distinct, over in Tuscany.

In many respects, Dante is a wonderful mirror for Mandelstam. Mandelstam recognizes in the *Comedy* a will to think time as "the contents of a history perceived as a unitary, synchronic act" – which requires the poetic mediated synchronization of events, names, and traditions that have been disjointed by the centuries. Just like the Russian poet, Dante "turns his nose up in front of flatly causal causality." Mandelstam also recognizes in the vast syncretism of the poem from Trecento (which constantly intertwines Greek and Roman history and the figures of saints, the origins of Christianity and the corrupt history of the papacy, the civil war in Florence and Hell) an imperative which is also his own: that of altering the structure of time and adopting poetic anachronism as a method.

He knows that the *Comedy* is nothing more than an immense vessel constructed by an exiled Dante in order to "take stock" and thus reconnect with his homeland beyond the banishment and discrediting. He admires the freedom and the richness of sight in which he views the other figures of knowledge from his time: theology, philosophy, science, politics, art, and love…. He perceives to what extent this thought is a living research and never the concretization of dead knowledge. He even describes it as a passionate will of "conducting experiments" *avant la lettre*. In the *Comedy*, he writes, "the eye is prepared to see new things." "[Dante] is not idle: he must develop a space open to the flow and remove the cataract of a hardened vision." And, his highest praise: "he writes dictation, he is a copyist, a translator."

In this sense, the *Comedy* is situated outside of literature as a finished product. Rather, it is the site of a constant mutation of the most precise and rebellious poetic matter: "Dante is the poet par excellence who shakes the sense and violates the integrity of the image." The noun "is the goal and not the subject of the sentence." It is impossible to grasp that Dante's poetic thought would proceed by way of developments. It is more a question of dealing with a "series of projectiles created as one goes along, each one soaring in succession in order to assure the continuity of movement itself." In such a way that the *Comedy*, "far from monopolizing the time of the reader, allows it to flourish." And, for Mandelstam, this is a major poetic virtue: Dante is "the strategist of transformations and crossbreedings" because for him it is always about rendering the "internal form of a structure and tension."

Reading Dante with the most extreme acuity, Mandelstam constantly talks about himself, and how his own poems work. He goes as far as speaking of walking – as a physical, rhythmical root of the verse – which he shares with the great Italian. Moreover, those who knew him highlight that it is his own portrait he is tracing when he writes: "The step, linked with breath and impregnated with thought, is [for Dante] the principle of prosody [...]. For him, philosophy and poetry are always moving, always on their feet."

He intimately recognizes in the Hell of the *Divine Comedy* not a fiction, but the city of Florence suffering – like Russia in the 1930s – from the political conflicts tearing it apart: "the city in the midst of love, passion, and hate," within "[the] most dangerous, intricate, and criminal century."

But Mandelstam also identifies a subjective posture that he shares with the Florentine banished from his city: a retreat into the limbo of a life without life, whence the poet looks at what comes out of this and persists, thinking and naming it without ever wanting to separate himself from it. No more so than Dante who couldn't tolerate being separated from Florence, merely conceiving of the *Comedy* as a path to lead him back there, with the confidence that his poem would bring him a complete victory over his contemporaries who slandered and forced him into exile.

This journey by Dante confirms Mandelstam within the negation of any oriented figure of time, of any history thought in terms of cause and effect. His intuition is that of an irreversible dismemberment by the event, of a temporal discontinuity that requires no longer thinking the present in regard to the past (which in no way would explain what there is), but on the contrary, in firmly projecting oneself into the unknown of the present.

This time that is split in two by History requires the poet to work for man to be "the firmest thing on the earth": "Man must be the firmest thing on the earth, and should regard his relation to the earth as diamond to glass" ("About the Nature of The Word").

In order to continue to touch the ground under these extreme conditions, the poem must first "turn up time so that the deep layers of time, its black soil region, appear on top"; but the poem must also be capable of tearing away the present moment, in its entirety, from the soil of time ("Word and Culture"). These two operations require a refined touch and a precision of absolute gestures: "The present moment can bear the weight of centuries, preserve its wholeness, and retain its 'now.' One only needs to know how to dig it out of the soil of time without damaging its roots – Otherwise it will wither" ("François Villon").

These operations require, from the poem, a form of interiority to science and a mode of interlocution with politics whose innovative intensity Mandelstam admires in the work of Dante. Mandelstam is greatly moved by, and profoundly shares in, the project of the *Comedy*: to take stock, as poet and through poems, of politics, science, theology, philosophy, art, and love. For the voyage of Dante in the *Comedy* is not a voyage into established forms of knowledge, but into the unknown: the tale of Ulysses (set to the Canto XXVI of the *Inferno*) returning to Ithaca and setting out again with his loyal seamen to as yet unknown seas where their boat will be swallowed up, stands for a secret image of Dante's own journey.

However, in contrast to the poetic matter of the *Comedy*, Mandelstam perceives that the poem has unlearned the art of describing lone realities "whose structure lends itself to poetic representation: impulses, intentions, oscillations." He issues this painful and anguished quote to his contemporaries: "What will become of our poetry, shamelessly distanced from science?" He urges them to learn to give voice and song to "scientific systems, political theories, just as [our] predecessors did with nightingales and roses" ("The Word and Culture").

When you read and re-read Mandelstam, one thing jumps out at you: poem after poem, it is impossible to make oneself an image out of the time in which he writes that would somewhat correspond to what we think we know about this time by other means such as history. To put it another way, his poems short-circuit what we believe we know. Thus, even today, they still produce something unknown, they continue a vision that has not yet reached us, and this is indeed why we persist in always approaching them with the feeling that they continue to live, and not at all as mere signs of survival, but as an unheard of power of naming.

So he is justified in writing, (shortly before his death between March 9 and March 19, 1937):

[…] And when I die, my service over,
To everyone alive a lifelong friend,
reply of the sky will echo
Deeper and higher in my cold breast.

In a text from 1915 comparing the deaths of Scriabin and Pushkin, Mandelstam analyzed the question of the death of the artist: "I can speak of Scriabin's death (whose burial, like that of Pushkin's, led to the "gathering of the Russian people and made the sun rise upon him") as the supreme act of his oeuvre. In my opinion, the death of the artist should not be excluded from the continuous chain of his oeuvre, on the contrary, it is the final link in the chain, the conclusion."

This conviction certainly determined his decision to write the first poem about Stalin, a decision around which Mandelstam's fate will truly pivot. In effect, this decision prepares the path of his own death as the final figure of his oeuvre when he will anonymously disappear, once again alone on the Russian earth, on a journey toward exile, but "already dead a second time." The persistence in depriving him of any means for working or living made him a dead man, a dead man within life, but nevertheless more alive than those who persecuted him. This dead man is not the figure of a martyr, or a sacrificial hero, but the affirmation of indestructible choices, where "the reply of the sky echoes."

IV. Pasolini:
no longer History,
but a "memorable consciousness of sun"

Pasolini also encounters the immense figure of Dante when, in writing "The Ashes of Gramsci," he decides to expose the poem to the crossroads of the politics and history of his time, and decides that his poetic language must then be capable of bearing "the rational, the logical, the historical." In a historical-political sequence – 1950s Italy – which is completely controlled by the State and the political parties (and in this sense is not too different from our own time period), Pasolini remains in a position which he describes as "the difficult, painful and even humiliating position of political independence – a position that cannot accept any historical and practical kind of ideology, and suffers because of this, as if it had a guilty conscious – because, as a consequence, this decision of political independence finds itself excluded from any action."

The choice of engaging in what Pasolini will call his "experimentalism" is not based on a desire toward formalist experimentation, but on the necessary overcoming [*traversée*] of this difficult relationship with his time and its dominant political conceptions and conflicts. One of Pasolini's first experimental operations is thus to reinvigorate the triplet and the hendecasyllable, which are the basis for the prosodic form of the *Divine Comedy*, but in order to carefully make them limp, in order to destroy every one of them in reactivating them. This is a way of marking a linguistic filiation, but above all, via the destruction of the prosodic institution, it is a way of producing a major discord between political consciousness and historical consciousness.

This work on prosody inherited from the *Comedy* comes from Pasolini's identification of Dante as opening the way, within the middle of the Italian language, to "all the possible utterances of a common language – different according to each social class, and good for the most varied of uses: familiar, commercial, bureaucratic, literary, theological, political. A written and oral language."

The deliberate choice of a plurality of styles, of the coexistence and clashing of the different linguistic registers, ends up being for him, as it is for the creator of the *Comedy*, "a path of love: physical and sentimental love for the phenomena of the world – and an intellectual love for their spirit: the history which will always make both of us stand, 'with our feelings, there where the world is being transformed.'"

In the poem, "The Ashes of Gramsci," which can be found in the collection bearing the same name, the tension becomes almost unbearable between this poet's desire for "there where the world is being transformed" and what his own existential experience reveals to him as far as the obsolescence of Marxist political categories is concerned.

The political consciousness backed by the Italian communist party and Gramscian Marxism is fundamentally a historical consciousness, organized according to recognized figures like class struggle, revolution, and the communist party. The authority, radiation, and consumption of these categories are concentrated into Gramsci's personality (whose ashes alone remain in the cemetery gardens of Rome where Pasolini is meditating). This Marxist vision of history and historical consciousness as possible foundations for a present politics is what Pasolini will dispute within the stupefying meditation that animates this poem.

First he tests it by way of his personal relationship with the local inner-city inhabitants of Rome where he lives. Of his intimate knowledge of the young proletarian from the countryside and the city, with which he has for a long time linked his desire. But he would doubtless have had neither the courage nor the strength to raise his voice on this point – at a moment when this vision was not only dominant but hegemonic – if he had not forged another possible paradigm of political subjectivity: that which his brother and his peers provided as an example ten years earlier at the height of fascism and the world war, in joining the Resistance.

I would like to highlight to what extent his brother, killed in the hideouts in the Julian Mountains, is an essential character of the Pasolinian poems. He haunts them; he will always be the dead youth whose gaze alone can bear true judgment on the situation that Pasolini strives to think. So it is that he intervenes abruptly, starting from the very first poems that examine a lifeless and helpless after-war. But he will re-emerge once again, in the middle of the 1960s, in order to tear apart the inherent hypocritical consensus for what Pasolini will describe as a new "Prehistory." In the painful poem from 1964 entitled "Victory," the young partisan, out of his tomb, "strives to grasp what is real within the real, with a passion that refuses any temerity or extremism." And even within a version of "Divine Mimesis" (the dark unfinished double of the *Divine Comedy*), the new Virgil guiding the poet who descends into Hell is none other than the partisan – with the face of someone condemned to death, heading toward the mountains, conserving "the hardness of his hope."

The poem that best describes what would be the instruction of this brother in his poems would no doubt be a poem from *Religion of My Time*, entitled "The Resistance and its Light":

Thus I came to the days of the Resistance
without knowing anything except style.
It was a style all of light,
memorable consciousness of sun.
It could never fade, even for an instant,

The essential is expressed in the following: for the poet, the lesson of the Resistance is unforgettable and definitive; what Pasolini perceived was a new "style" of political action, and this style, as the poet then hammers out, is "pure light" or "memorable consciousness of sun." Why "pure?" Because it is not inferred from any objective condition, it does not emanate from a group, or express the interests or will of a certain class; it does not obey a directive. It is a solitary, unconditional, personal decision. This is what a poem from 1954, "Meeting," indicates with force, where the character of Guido comes to help the poet during his revolting confrontation with a neo-fascist meeting in the middle of Rome:

[…] my brother smiles at me,
close to me. He has, painful and shining
in his smile, light that makes him see,
obscure partisan that was not yet 20 years-old, in which direction he must choose

with a true dignity, with a rage exempt
from hate, our new history […]
Is it toward him, too honest,

too pure, to move on with a lowered head?
Beg for a bit of light for
this world resuscitated an obscure morning?

Here, the word "light" denotes once again the disinterested implementation of hope, which is of the order of a principle – which expresses, in the preceding poem, the reference to Justice (with a capital J):

This light was hope of justice:
I didn't know which kind: Justice.

But this same poem – it is essential to read the poem in this manner in order to compare it to the kernel of anxiety found in "The Ashes of Gramcsi" – then attempts to link this unheard of style of political engagement to the emergence of a completely different figure, who emerged, from the countryside of Frioul, with agricultural workers struggling with the landowners: "the day laborers who fought."

Moved by this movement of poor farm workers, Pasolini, regarding their struggle, registers a substantial modification to what he had called "pure light." Even if "light is always equal to another light," Pasolini judges that it undergoes an alteration: "from light, it becomes an uncertain daybreak."

The transformation of solar light into an "uncertain daybreak" indicates that the historical future from then on bears upon this new figure of political subjectivity, determining decisions and contents: the light of daybreak only has a value in becoming the announcement of the day to come. With the day laborers in struggle, one goes from the domain of pure principle – always both a contemporary of the present and unconditional (Pasolini will call it "eternal") – to the history of class struggle, which is to say, to actions arising from, articulated on, the determination of a future. If historical consciousness, the consciousness of class struggle, can be called a "new light" – which is what these lines indicate:

> In history, justice was conscious
> of a human division of riches,
> and hope took on a new light,

however, this light is no longer exactly within the register of what had been stated as the "memorable consciousness of sun":

> the nascent daybreak was a light
> outside of the eternity of style....

The will of justice from then on finds itself indexed on objective parameters: social classes, their antagonistic interests, external to the principle of the field – "outside of the eternity of style."

Thus, according to this poem, there are two possible states of light: two figures of political subjectivity whose internal energy sources are absolutely not the same, and which enter into conflict by way of Pasolini's apprehension for certain circumstances, granting him a superior and anticipating lucidity, but also opening up a violent anxiety within him.

The poem "The Ashes of Gramsci" begins by the diagnosis that the 1950s in Italy are a time of "deathly peace, disquieting," in which a lifestyle arose that would be better termed survival rather than living. History is from then on empty; sensuality alone permeates a world that all ideals have deserted:

> The emptier each
>
> ideal – in this vacuum of history,
> in this buzzing pause when life is silent –
> the more obvious the awesome,
> almost Alexandrian
> sensuality, which impurely decorates
> all with golden light

"I'm not speaking of the individual," Canto V insists. "That phenomenon of sensual and sentimental passions ..." is not that of the poet who, on the contrary, lives by way of "eluding life," and in his heart "the feeling grows of a life becoming grieving / violent oblivion."

This passion – that he perceives, analogically, in Shelley's caprice which swallowed him up "in the dazzling turquoise of the Tyrrhenian Sea" – emanates from the entirety of Italy, foremost from these "young men with tan sweaty faces" for whom:

> [...] everywhere the boundless
> percussion instrument of sex and light
> buzzes joyfully [...]

Such conditions challenge the category of history itself. Such is the distraught intuition that is evoked throughout the long exploration of the poem.

The world in which history was alive was a world that was politically divided. In its contradictory structure, the resting place for Gramsci's remains bears witness to this – the somber "*acattolico*" cemetery of Rome. The "bones of millionaires / from mightier nations," are "the still-not dispersed seeds / of their ancient domination [...] possessed by a greed / that buries its grandeur and abomination / deep in the centuries"; whereas, encircling their tombs, and "attesting to its end," "the striking of anvils, stifled, softly" comes from the humble Testaccio quarter (a neighborhood of ateliers, repair shops, and slaughterhouses).

Pasolini does not challenge this objective division of the world. Quite to the contrary: the way in which he lives in Rome during those years, "poor among the poor," makes him aware that the one thing that sets him apart is "possessing" history, namely being conscious of this division, this splitting of the world into antagonistic social classes.

But Pasolini's knowledge of the "proletarian life" that surrounds him, pitilessly warns him that history is no longer what animates this life, and that it is illusory to think that political subjectivity can still have as its source social classes and their struggle. History, in a certain way, has passed on to the other side, since it can also be expressed as "the most exalting / bourgeois possession of all." History participates with forms of knowledge and is no

62

longer a possible principle for thinking action or rebellion. The existence of social classes and their struggle henceforth no longer has the status of a real political source "for these weak people,", but the status of myth.

What the people of the Roman suburbs possess for themselves can be summed up by their bare lives, "the untrustworthy expansive gift of existence," the joy that they can draw from their "corporeal collective presence," where the "lack of any true religion" can be felt. Popular nihilism: this life alone "fills their hearts" and "those lost in it, serenely lose it [...]."

Furthermore, Pasolini proves that he is no different than them concerning this point, that he lives like everyone "in non-will," within a non choice, or within the impossibility of choosing from then on.

Concerning this point, the poet must dare to proclaim what he knows: that "our history is finished," and that there can no longer be a history that would still be "our" history. "The ideal that gives light," the Marxist ideal is like the image of Gramsci's ashes, "buried in earth / foreign, still banished." The ashes of the Marxist philosopher, in front of which Pasolini meditates, are also the ashes of the historicist conception of political action.

A truth which rips him apart, precisely because he has "the conscious heart / of one who can only live within history."

A scandalous and painful truth, foremost for himself, in his encounter with Gramsci:

The scandal of contradicting myself, of being
With you and against you; with you in my heart,
in light, but against you in the dark viscera;
but a truth he experienced in its most deepest.

From here the poem opens up to the unknown. For if we do not renounce the idea that the world is divided, then what do we still base political decision on if it is no longer based on historical consciousness?

A vast number of questions still remain that are barely elucidated or shared because they challenge the entire apparatus of the parties and their connection to the State, every vision of the political action that is foremost founded on the State and its requisites, values, and order. If politics is no longer expressive of a history or a class, if it no longer refers to objectivity, how does one think it within the element of "pure light," which is the anticipation of the Pasolinian paradigm?

In the 1970s, Pasolini will once again affirm with the same force and anxiety that the conception of a unique world is also the (dangerous) imposition on everyone by the State of a single present. "I descend into hell," he writes, "and I know things that threaten the peace of others. But watch out. Hell is rising toward us. It is true that it comes bearing a mask...." Masked, among other things, by the consensual confusion between development and progress, by the ideology of tolerance, a corollary of a society that has never been more intolerant.... This is strictly what he tries to describe under the name of a "new fascism" backed by school, television, and newspapers: "the great preservers of this horrible life, founded on the idea of possessing and destroying." And he will also call it – which garners him much hatred – "the protective classicism, that characterizes / the politically correct communist":

who makes himself the slave of his enemy, who goes
where the enemy goes, under the guidance of history
which is both their history, and which in the end, strangely makes
them the same.

The poet's discovery of the obsolescence of the category of history, "when it has been quite a long time now that the people no longer anthropologically exists," sheds light on Pasolini's distrust in the student movements resulting from 1968, to which he addresses this perspicacious question:

They march with their flags and slogans,
but what separates them from "power?"

Whether it is by way of his poems or films, as poet, he will never renounce exposing a real that is constantly heading toward suppression, and whose existence is hidden and denied by the state political categories. And he does so with some success as this following remark by Fortini about the film *Accattone* bears witness:

64

Yesterday evening I told myself: I don't personally know this world. If I had to frequent it, I would experience repugnance and fear. And nevertheless, the film portrays it as a comprehensible, fraternal, and human world – a world which belongs, or has belonged, to my biographical experience and which it is possible to communicate with.

"Change, in a way that be just as radical and hopeless as the situation is." And: "Go on claiming, desiring, identifying yourself with what is other, keeping imperturbably, obstinately, eternally adverse; scandalizing; blaspheming."

Do not these two major imperatives for Pasolini still hold true for us?

V. The "Misty" Poets:

thinking while propped up against the empty sites of History and language.

The generation of the "Menglong" poets appeared in China in the aftermath of the Cultural Revolution. I owe my reading of these poets mostly to Italian-English translations of their poems thanks to my two Italian friends, Claudia Pozzana and Alessandro Russo (two sinologists and great connoisseurs of 20th century Chinese politics and history as well as prominent translators of contemporary Chinese poets). To this day, very few of these poets have been translated into French.

The publication in 1978 of the independent journal *Jintian* (which means "Today") by two of these poets, Mang Ke and Bei Dao, was a formative event in Beijing. The journal was first plastered on the walls surrounding the university and then distributed by hand in the city center. It was a question of providing readers with an entirely new poetic production that knew it couldn't officially be published in China.

The founding experience of these poets is double: on one hand, there is the Cultural Revolution that they had experienced and which some of them had taken part in (for example as young students spending time working in the countryside), which stands behind them as an enigmatic void, an event whose assessment remains largely indecipherable and even difficult or impossible to think.

"Homage to Poetry," one of Yang Lian's first poems, describes this situation:

In the anonymous instant
The wind boat bearing history has passed
inside me – like a shadow
an end follows me

But on the other hand, that this obscure, opaque event adheres to what they are, does not mean that one should renounce or invalidate it. These poets will, on the contrary, lean against it like a chasm, but also like a nameless site where it will be a question of thinking and reconstituting an entire space with intellectuality.

Looking back at these years during the Cultural Revolution, Gu Cheng writes: "It was as if the Earth once again separated itself from the Sky, as if, for an instant, we experienced the innocent age of humanity." There are historical circumstances in which the powers that are set in motion and the human stakes are such that they are *terrestrial events*, in the sense of events that fracture the earth of men. A sentiment echoed in the following lines from Nerval's "Myrtho", and which for me, show the parallels between these two poets:

I know why the volcano over there has re-opened....
Because yesterday you had grazed it with you nimble foot,
And the horizon was suddenly covered with ash

After years of vivid words of all kinds ("The Cultural Revolution," Zhai Yongming writes, "transformed popular masses into poets of the proletarian revolution"), in the 1980s, the language of politics becomes completely locked down by the language of the State. Then to take up speech in poems requires finding a way to escape this complete imprisonment within the language of the State, to undo the adhesion to its words and names that have become untruthful and inert.

Meng Lang reflects on this situation in terms that seem extraordinary to me in every way: "Poets," he writes, "hover within the blind spots of history. Someone with a historical viewpoint cannot see these sites. The existence of the blind spots of history has only been discovered by humanity in the 20th century. These sites have been discovered by the poets. [...] Poets are worried 'from the inside,' and that's how it should be."

These poets "worried from the inside" are not only considered along with the State and with its language, but with history, which, as soon as politics becomes absent, fuses itself with the State. If there is no longer history other than that of the State, to think outside the field of the State implies identifying and viewing those empty spaces or blind spots about which Meng Lang speaks.

Here I will also cite Bei Dao concerning this point:

> History is a void
> A continuing genealogical register
> Only the dead can obtain recognition

From then on, not only does history belong to the dead and no longer to the living, but as State history, it weighs as a burden on all of Chinese intellectual life: "The poet must strive to solve the problem of this burden," Bei Dao writes. Because for Bei Dao, there is no question of renouncing the search for light:

> The dark night has given me dark eyes
> But I use them in order to find the moon

This is why the first public appearance of these poets will be focused around a very simple line by Bei Dao, but which had the effect of an intellectual thunderbolt: "I don't believe."

> I tell you, world
> I-don't-believe!
> I don't believe the sky is blue
> I don't believe in the echo of your notes....

This speech, which has forever opened philosophy, in its inaugural and methodical refusal of opinion, is taken up here as the poet's speech. For all philosophy is absent in China during this time period. And in these circumstances, as Xi Chuan emphasizes: "poetry is the philosophy of the poets."

The refusal to believe in history accompanies the refusal to believe in a language that has been linked and occupied by the language of the State for thousands of years.

One must listen to the warning expressed by Yang Lian: "Each Chinese character is a trap into which the entirety of each generation has fallen." As well as the warning of Gu Cheng: "I have discovered a strange phenomenon: written characters move all by themselves, they go in several directions or vanish into thin air. One must have a lot of time in order to find the possible word. Arbitrary alterations of these characters are dangerous, they present intonations and effects that are not justified."

How does one master these characters? For these poets, it is not a question of finding, like it was for Mandelstam, the "senseless" name of the epoch, but of finding the "possible" word in order to be sure of simply speaking with their own mouths.

How can the Chinese language open itself back up to truth? In the poem, "Reply," Bei Dao describes the dual pressure that is exerted on this commitment:

> Five thousand years of pictograms
> and the eyes of the men of the future look at us.

Gu Cheng, for his part, describes their solitude within a time where he himself feels "isolated from everything like an iron vase," "without anyone being capable of receiving help from culture, history, or the external world."

Some of these poets will compare their attempts to that of Dante, which in my mind is deserved. In order to think his epoch for himself (and not in the terms offered by philosophy, theology, politics, science, art, or the love of his time), it was vital for Dante to create a new language and to separate his own language from Latin, the language of authority. In the same manner, these Chinese poets will attempt to produce a new language, according to completely novel methods and means. The great intellectual Chinese movement at the beginning of the 20th century invented what was called "*baihua*," or "clear language" – a spoken language that aimed to replace "*wenyan*," which was the written language of the Empire. Science, literature, and politics would be written in this new language, and at the same time, would lead to a considerable amount of translation work.

However, the Chinese socialist years saw the abandonment of this research which was replaced by a dialectical vision of art in the service of the politics of the State and the Chinese communist party.

Contrary to the modernist generation, the "Menglong" poets will not abandon the ancient language of poetry, but will attempt to reintroduce it in order to rework and displace it. This is the reason why the name "menglong" – which means "hazy or misty" (or more specifically: "clear-obscure," because the word denotes a semi-obscurity that is irradiated by a veiled light) – had ironically been attributed to them. A name which they took back up on their own account: for, all in all, their work in reintroducing a thought into the interior of the great poetic-state language could be represented as light attempting to pierce a thick and intense obscurity.

Indeed, in ancient Chinese poetry each sign, each character corresponds to a meaning; any possible void is filled in with an allusion, and language is presented as having an all-powerful, total signifying capacity. The Misty poets will strive to make their voices heard indicating that this is not at all the case, that quite to the contrary, in their own experience of language, as with history and politics, there are empty sites entirely withdrawn from signification and meaning.

By way of this movement, they also attempt a limitless appropriation of the Chinese literary past, not according to a regressive modality, but with, on the contrary, the will to head toward a non-reactive future.

From the 1980s to the 1990s, this small group of poets shared the strong conviction that it was up to them to sketch out, and even be, an "other China." For example, Yang Lian was capable of writing: "Chinese culture is what I'm striving to create, it is what I struggle to create every day – whether or not I'm in exile in regard to 'Cultural China.'" For the "root of culture is its opening to individual energies." "When I say we are creating a language for ourselves, what I mean is that we abandon the readymade ideas and concepts that have been transmitted to us by way of public discourse. We are trying to open up language to our own inclinations and desires, our own feelings. Until now, language has been closed off to me. But, we cannot speak of anything – thoughts, feelings, experiences – without there first existing a language in which we can share all these things."

Each of these poets concentrated themselves on the task of making existence appear as a powerful figure in his own register, not under the guise of an individualism – in the Western sense of the term – but as a site that one had to make emerge, within its own positivity, as a reality distinct from the reality of the State and history.

Gu Cheng declares as much:

I don't represent history
I don't represent the voice
that comes from on high
I came here merely by way of the age that is mine.

I cannot make use of the plume
nor the inkwell
only the use of
the most leisurely breath of life
may inscribe
a trace upon which it is worth making a conjecture
("Farewell, Tomb")

To make the power of individuality and existence emerge requires lyricism, but for these poets, it is not a romantic lyricism. For them, lyricism (like the supreme poetic fiction according to Stevens) must possess a strong capacity of abstraction: as for what constitutes existence, it is not a question of pouring one's heart out, but thinking.

For Bei Dao, for example, the poem is the site that stabilizes a world, "a sincere and unique world, a world of justice and humanity." It is vital for him to construct such a world if we want to prevent the risk of the annihilating dispersion that the infinite multiplicity of things and experiences represent.

Existence, life, is posited as "poetry's other." An "other" that is of the same order as the "what is other" around which Pasolini instructs one to identify with. For example, if it is a question of confronting love, a triple capacity is required of the poem: a cold indifference ("withdraw oneself from all fervor, all impulse"), distance (the refusal of pathos), and indirectness ("saying something directly is too simple").

This new lyricism rejects any social or political function of language. The singular power of language is not of this register, as Bei Dao accentuates in a poem that I cited in the introduction of this book:

Many languages
Fly through this world
But the production of language
Can neither increase nor diminish
The silent pain of humanity

For his part, Yang Lian relies on the singularity of the Chinese language in order to shield it from the pressure of historical time and to open up within it the question of a "now" that must always be constructed: "Unlike European languages that strive to capture the concrete, Chinese is abstract through and through. Pronouns can be omitted, and there is no distinction of time, or the singular or plural. And a Chinese sentence does not describe "movements" but "situations" [...]. Poetic space becomes deprived of any temporal particularity."

This absence of time inherent to the Chinese language can be turned into an open receptivity to all times, to the production of a syncretism in which the world and subject will no longer be separated. "The real is part of my nature," Yang Lian declares. Poetry once again becomes possible if the poet can affirm that his operations upon words are indeed operations upon existence, if the poem can be deemed "the lone site for resurrection."

"Language disappears on water," " the wind sweeps away ideograms," but the position of the word within the poem is not representative or denotative; the word co-belongs to the world.

Far from repeating life, poetry "corrects," according to Bei Dao, and in so doing, in return, life "corrects the echo of poetry" ("Requiem"). For it is life that is the echo of poetry, not the inverse. Here we find a thought that is akin to that of Stevens. Within this configuration, as Yang Lian remarks with acuity, "it is the poem that writes the poet."

By way of the Misty poets we have the remarkable invention of an "impersonal lyricism" – I will risk this oxymoron – in which the personal existence of the poet bears and attests to the uprising of a world.

VI. Aygi:

the poem of a world without particularities

Aygi presented himself as one of the successors of the poets he called "rebel poets (or poets of resistance)": examples include Mandelstam and Celan. With Mandelstam and Celan (and in another sense, Pasolini), it appears that poetry has reached its limits in relation to history. For his part, Aygi is convinced that poetry cannot begin to exist again if it doesn't assume an innocence, and in order for this to happen, poetry must reject any link with history or extreme situations.

In 1990, he writes:

> Silent spiritual resistance is normal and legitimate in order to preserve one's self as a man, to preserve one's human dignity and convictions, one's spiritual interests; but the art that it has generated also bears within itself a principle of self-destruction. Resistance destroys, it leads people in a desperate opposition with something, and this war for survival is, despite whatever we say about it, a factor of internal destruction. In a general manner, fighting against any power whatsoever (not historically, but currently), against Brezhnev, or anyone else, is sterile for literature and art: they degenerate. In such a situation, to say the word "fight" is to already admit defeat.

This is in agreement with the diagnosis of Mo Mo, one of the Misty poets, who writes: "Revolution and destruction are still the main themes of poetry. Poetry is still not yet on the path of creation and construction."

From the beginning, Aygi is in search of an affirmative poetry, free to speak starting from itself and not from what it has to combat. One could also say: a radically non-dialectical poetry. In no way does this mean that Aygi seeks refuge in his "ego," within the expression of his own personality. Nor does it mean he turns his back on his time.

On the contrary, his hope and ambition is to return the world to men in its entirety: through himself, the poet must express the world, and fully affirm "the connection of man with nature, his freedom and responsibility in the world." This will is strongly reminiscent of Hölderlin's project during the French Revolution. "The art of the future that is free, harmonious, and constructive" supposes a return to a primary innocence. Aygi's singular method for returning there is to construct each poem in such a way that each thing taken from the world irradiates a universal light. In his poems, each thing inscribed is, if I can put it like this, a "color" of universality. And this can first of all be said in regard to the sites and landscape of Chuvashia: the fields, forests, wind, snow, roses, or the flowers with magical names such as the phlox....

In 1985, he said to his translator, Leon Robel:

> I was born in a Chuvash village, surrounded by thick, immense forest; the windows of our little isba gave us a direct view of the fields, field and forest constituted "my entire universe." When I discovered through world literature "ocean-worlds," "city-worlds" of other people, I forced myself to not let my "Forest-Field" world become diminished in its literary significance in relation to the other universally known "worlds" and in the same way – insofar as it is possible – my world would acquire a certain "general value." I wanted to raise the "small" into the Largest. And so it was that "my" fields and forest appeared, that my "snow" appeared, whitening out everything all the way to the symbol.

Agyi's poetry is a poetry where nothing exists within the mode of the particular, even though it is born out of these perfectly defined and singular places that are the Chuvash landscapes. This seems to me to be its most fascinating and surprising characteristic. For this absence of particularity has nothing to do with abstraction. It is very different than what one experiences when one reads Mallarmé, for example, whose poems strive to produce a "pure Concept."

Aygi himself provides a name for the effects of his poems: "simplicity," or even "simpleness." It seems to me that these names

76

signify: each singular thing in the world can be perceived beyond its particularities as having a universal value, and men should relate to themselves and the entire universe on this specific mode or plane.

This desire for universality in Aygi is not a philosophical desire, but a poetic desire. Have a look at "Silence of Snow" from 1985 that belongs to the beautiful collection, *Child-And-Rose*:

> without beginning
> within time
> from nowhere they are
> without peaceable roots
> free
> without having in particular in general
> without defining semblance or place
> neither being knowable or possible
> oh simply they exist they are
> within this unique peace
> silence

Aygi sometimes gives to this existence of the present universality in flower and fields, roads and the woods, in the wind and snow, in childhood and sleep, the name of God. But this God of the poems is not identifiable to the gods of Religion. "God" is most often the name of a poetic state of the world and the things within the world: moments where grace is granted to us in order to see them shine in all their affirmative radiance.

This state appears or reveals itself, when the poem succeeds in creating a new kind of silence – a silence in which all false and particular meanings bonded by words onto the world disappear and things can then emerge within the luminous radiance that is all their own, in their "simplicity" or "simpleness." The "World-Noise," as an interview from 1985 states, "begins to sometimes appear as a Pseudo-World – who will wash it clean until arriving at silence? Perhaps from now on, art alone. One must not merely 'enter into a relation with silence.' Apparently from now on in poetry, it is necessary to know how to create silence." Sleep or early childhood are privileged materials of the poem, because they are close to this kind of silence that the poem must know how to produce, a silence anterior to particularizing meanings.

One could say that Aygi's poems whisper. Because their extreme sophistication is a way to subtract the verse from any noise that any rhetoric inevitably makes, subtracting them *a priori* from any syntax.

The poem must in effect constitute by itself "a kind of general sign" – allowing for the most concrete signs of its contents to shine through: "When I want to emphasize [these signs], I italicize them, or in separating the letters, I sometimes introduce hieroglyphics or ideograms, particularly individualized 'blank spaces' (they, like the signs, each time have a particular 'meaning')."

The poet makes use of signs of punctuation in order to recompose, combine anew, a syntax in which a group of words, for example, counts as a singular new word. Such is the case in the beginning of this poem, among many others, from 1997 titled, "Fields of this Summer":

> and even here
> time seems to tremble – again renewing
> these farewell-fields –
>
> (like peoplefarewells) –

The world does not dominate us, for we are the world. But this only becomes true or possible if, "in-the-world-as-action," we are capable of consecrating time to "serving silence." How does one inscribe, within the substance of the poem, the marks of one's effort to tend to silence? The poem must never say too much. As soon as something has truly been said, the poem must cut it short, the line must be interrupted: "I'm striving more and more for a single poem to, in one way or another, be capable of representing *silence* itself."

For Aygi, each poem also exists as a singularity, better yet: an individuality. It stands up by itself. This is why, like a human being, the poem has a name (its title) and a date of birth.

In 1992, in "Poetry as Silence," he writes: "And until then – ever further – into the snows. Into naked poverty. How few things were needed. Hands – only a little more. A poem ... – all so little, all more and more – without us – the World."

Elsewhere he writes ("Always Farther in the Snow," 1986-1987):

The snow
works in the fields
(a true poet more modest than a poet)

Here snow is the image of the true poet because snow gives the landscape its whiteness, its absence of colors and particularities, thus revealing the universality present in the world. Snow is more modest than the poet because it does not need words in order to erase particularisms and makes the universality visible within things.

A "Breath of Fraternity" ("The last ravine / Paul Celan," 1983, dedicated to Martine Broda), such is the relationship the poem strives to maintain with the real. Men should strive to learn to see the world as it is shown in the poem for themselves: "insubstantial specter of some eternity" ("Definitive Departure," August, 1988, Budapest).

In the work of Caeiro, the intervention of the poet is para-doxical: he is always this "odious thing," an interpreter of Nature. Ideally, for Aygi as well, the poet should be absent. Poetic work is only justified if it is able to create within us a freedom for seeing beyond the details, if it grants us another foundation within the world. This is exactly what one of his last poems wonderfully de-scribes, "Again the fields before sleep":

Within the noise
Within the radiance! —

more and more pure – clean – transparent
these spaces alone – soar:

(one could say – through everything: through the forests –
through the buildings – through the clouds) –

they alone: "speak" – "love" – "play" – "become sad" –

"in a word" – rejoice! –

and with no need for "details"... –

as if to us also they whispered
in order for us to think clearly:
do we ("at least") when we die – carry with us "details" –

(we depart – purely)

(2003)

This poem confirms a decisive poem from 1958, titled "Here,"
where Aygi reports how one day he began to perceive the word
"here" as a veritable hieroglyph of existence. "Here" is all that we
possess, for:

it signifies the earth and the sky
and what is in the shadows
and what we see with our own eyes
and that which I can only share in verse

But "here" does not signify limits. It does not express a finitude.
For it is here that we possess immortality:

the secret of immortality is not higher up than the secret
of a bush illuminated by a winter's night
than the white-branches above the snow
than the dark shadows upon the snow

In this sense, I will argue that Aygi is the poet of our true contemporary metaphysical freedom. His poems outline the elevated figure of a being in the world capable of having a relation with any
singularity and existence as a possible support, a peaceful radiance
expressing the power of the universal. His most profound theme
is that only this figure can grant us the capacity of fraternally living on earth, which is our unique site.

In these days and years, where one must endure a country
coming undone from the inside, where persecutions based on
particularities and details proliferate, these poems must become
more precious and dear to us each time we encounter them.

VII. Leopardi:

the invention of the earth as the possible site of a collective without transcendence

Leopardi: both widely neglected (in France) and the object of a fierce conflict bearing on the very content of his poetry itself. A conflict between those who would see him swallowed up by a pathetic Romanticism, which is quite foreign to him, and those who would grant him a materialism and lucidity worthy of Lucretius, while seeing him as a cynic and skeptic, as his century's "libertine."

This debate is still open, for it is far from having been settled. And although he may be a contemporary of Romanticism, Leopardi is an intense "stranger" of a poet – and in this respect he is like Kleist, both of whom seem to have taken Mandelstam's program to heart in advance: "To exchange signals with Mars [...] is a task worthy of a lyric poet" ("About an Interlocutor").

In Leopardi's case, "Infinitive," and "The Broom" are enough to make him the nineteenth century creator of the "earth," which, one century later, Stevens would say should become poetry's principal referent. Recall his statement that "The great poems of heaven and hell have been written and the great poem of the earth remains to be written" (*The Necessary Angel*).

The site of Leopardi's thought is one of retreat. Recanati's poet is a poet "in retreat," like Emily Dickinson shutting herself off in her family home, or Hölderlin in the tower of Tübingen where he spent the second half of his life. It is not by chance that I bring these three figures together, and it is, to my mind, crucial to circulate between them. In these three lives, retreat is not an empirical

81

situation; nor is it even – despite appearances – a figure imposed by existence. Above all, retreat in no way expresses an ignorance or detachment from the configurations of action and time. To the contrary, it is retreat that allows, that creates, the distance necessary to imagine and think against the current of dominant visions.

One poem, "The Solitary Life," describes the state that evokes, for Leopardi, retreat's unhurried movement:

> From time to time I sit in solitude
> Upon the sloping border of a lake,
> A lake engarlanded with silent growth.
> Therein, with noonday wheeling through the sky,
> The sun is able to reflect his face,
> No blade of grass or leaf bends in the wind,
> And not only surface wrinkle, one cicada
> Clicking, one feather lifted on the bough,
> Or fluttering butterfly, or voice or motion,
> Nearby or distant, can be heard or seen.
> The deepest stillness dominates those banks;
> Almost I lose myself and all the world,
> I stay so still; it really seems my limbs
> Are now so loose and slack no sense or spirit
> Can move them more, their immemorial stillness
> Merged in that place and in its silences.

What is striking, at the beginning of this poem, is how the sought-after state under the noonday's solar flare, is a state that sensation and thought may liken to a corpse's tranquil rest. As if to lucidly confront the proof of life's nonsense, we must come very close to non-life.

Along its trajectory, the poem nevertheless marks a displacement: from broad daylight to the depths of night. And this transpires with the adoption of the moon (that "benevolent queen of the night"), whose cold nocturnal light suits the one for whom "all sweetness has grown strange," because he has renounced, not just love, but the very hope of love: "you will see me often, lonely, mute, / Wander through woods and by the verdant shores, / Or sit upon the grass, happy enough / If heart and breath are left to me to sigh." So begin the long years during which the moon is Leopardi's only interlocutor.

"To Count Carlo Pepoli" forms the hypothesis that the day shall come when the poet shall give up even more, the day when even emotion and beauty shall be refused to him:

> And when this breast to all things has become
> Insensible and cold, nor the sweet smile
> And rest profound of lonely sun-lit plains,
> Nor cheerful morning song of birds in spring,
> Nor moonlight soft, that rests on hills and fields,
> Beneath the limpid sky, will move my heart;
> When every beauty, both of Nature, and
> Of Art, to me will be inanimate
> And mute; each tender feeling, lofty thought,
> Unknown and strange; [...]
> The bitter truth must I investigate,
> The destinies mysterious, alike
> Of mortal and immortal things;
> [...] And if, at times,
> The truth discussing, my opinions should
> Unwelcome be, or not be understood,
> I shall not grieve, indeed, because in me
> The love of fame will be extinguished quite;
> Of fame, that idol frivolous and blind;
> More blind by far than Fortune, or than Love.

The poem "The Broom" (also known as "The Flower of the Desert") will study "the blind fate of mortal and eternal things," but in "Infinitive" it is the bitter truth that is at stake. This poem is built on a vertiginous contrast between the hedge that bounds the horizon, the mark that human finitude has left upon the countryside, and the limitless infinity of the universe that exists beyond that hedge. The sense of the immensity and unlimited multiplicity of worlds, of their incommensurability, placed side by side with the tiny and senseless character of "the human seasons," completed, or rather extended, by a luxurious shipwreck.

Here, I will provide the original, along with three dissimilar translations of the poem.

Sempre caro mi fu quest'ermo colle,
E questa siepe, che da tanta parte
Dell'ultimo orizzonte il guardo esclude.
Ma sedendo e mirando, interminati
Spazi di là da quella, e sovrumani
Silenzi, e profondissima quiete
Io nel pensier mi fingo ; ove per poco
Il cor non si spaura. E come il vento
Odo stormir tra queste piante, io quello
Infinito silenzio a questa voce
Vo comparando : e mi sovvien l'eterno,
E le morte stagioni, e la presente
E viva, e il suon di lei. Così tra questa
Immensità s'annega il pensier mio :
E il naufragar m'è dolce in questo mare.

Jaccottet's translation:

Toujours j'aimai cette hauteur déserte
Et cette haie qui du plus lointain horizon
Cache au regard une telle étendue.
Mais demeurant et contemplant j'invente
Des espaces interminables au-delà, de surhumains
Silences et une si profonde
Tranquillité que pour un peu se troublerait
Le coeur. Et percevant
Le vent qui passe dans ces feuilles – ce silence
Infini, je le vais comparant
À cette voix, et me souviens de l'éternel,
Des saisons qui sont mortes et de celle
Qui vit encor, de sa rumeur. Ainsi
Dans tant d'immensité ma pensée sombre,
Et m'abîmer m'est doux en cette mer.

I've always loved this lonesome hill
And this hedge that hides
The entire horizon, almost, from sight.
But sitting here in a daydream, I picture
The boundless spaces away out there, silences
Deeper than human silence, an unfathomable hush
In which my heart is hardly a beat
From fear. And hearing the wind
Rush rustling through these bushes,
I pit its speech against infinite silence –
And a notion of eternity floats to mind,
And the dead seasons, and the season
Beating here and now, and the sound of it. So,
In this immensity my thoughts all drown;
And it's easeful to be wrecked in seas like these.[1]

---

1. "Infinitive." trans. Eamon Grennan. Leopardi: Selected Poems. Princeton: Princeton University Press, 1997. p. 3.

The translation by Bonnefoy (in 18 lines, as opposed to the 15 contained in the original, and one caesura):

Toujours chère me fut cette colline
Solitaire ; et chère cette haie
Qui refuse au regard tant de l'ultime
Horizon de ce monde. Mais je m'assieds,
Je laisse aller mes yeux, je façonne, en esprit,
Des espaces sans fin au-delà d'elle,
Des silences aussi, comme l'humain en nous
N'en connaît pas, et c'est une quiétude
On ne peut plus profonde : un de ces instants
Où peu s'en faut que le coeur ne s'effraie.
Et comme alors j'entends
Le vent bruire dans ces feuillages, je compare
Ce silence infini à cette voix,
Et me revient l'éternel en mémoire
Et les saisons défuntes, et celle-ci
Qui est vivante, en sa rumeur. Immensité
En laquelle s'abîme ma pensée,
Naufrage, mais qui m'est doux dans cette mer.

Always this hill was
Dear to me
Solitary, and dear this hedge
Refusing the gaze the final
Horizon of this world. But I sit,
I let my eyes wander, I fix,
In my my mind,
Endless spaces beyond it
Silences as well, that the human in us
Does not know, and it is a tranquil peace
There is nothing more profound: one of these instants
Where little is needed to frighten the heart.
And as I hear
The wind rustling in the leaves, I compare
This infinite silence to this voice,
And I remember again the notion of the eternal
And the seasons gone-by, and this season
Alive, by way of its rumbling. This immensity
In which my thoughts drown,
So calmly shipwrecked in seas like these.

And the translation by Jean-Charles Vegliante:

Toujours cher me fut ce côteau isolé,
et cette haie qui interdit au regard
tant de parties d'un horizon plus lointain.
Mais assis devant cette vue, des espaces
au-delà sans limites, de surhumains
silences, la tranquillité très-profonde
je forme en ma pensée ; à quoi, pour un peu,
s'effraierait le coeur. Et comme j'entends bruire
le vent parmi ces plantes-ci, le silence
infini là-bas, je le compare encore
à cette voix : et me revient l'éternel,
et les saisons mortes, et puis la présente
et vive, et le son d'elle. Ainsi parmi cette
immensité ma pensée va s'engloutir :
et le naufrage m'est doux dans cette mer.

This lonesome hill has always been dear to me,
And this hedge which forbids to the gaze
So many aspects of the distant horizon.
But seated in front of this view,
Limitless spaces beyond, superhuman
Silences, the most-profound tranquility
In my mind I form; that, in its smallness,
Which would trouble the heart. And as I hear
The wind rustling among the plants, the infinite
Silence, there, I compare it again to this voice: and the eternal
Returns to my mind,
And these dead seasons, and then the sound of the present, alive.
Among this immensity my thought shall sink,
A shipwreck, so sweet to me in this sea.

The poem brushes up against a Pascalian statement: "I am frightened by the silence of infinite spaces" in order to take flight with the flap of a wing. The infinitude of the universe, in which thought is shipwrecked, plummeted, or engulfed is not, for Leopardi, cause for destitution or anxiety. Quite the contrary, the affect that belongs to this thought is one of sweetness. That is what is so extraordinary about this poem: if sweetness prevails over dread (trouble, as translated by Jaccottet), it is because this impossible thought, the thought of the universe's infinitude, is nevertheless possible because it is a thought that has been forged by man. Finite though he may be, man has something of the infinite about him, since he is capable of thinking the infinite's infinitude.

The luxurious shipwreck is not a flight or a retreat when confronted with the thought of the infinite, but rather a confident surrender to it. Even if the hedge closes in upon the horizon, even if vision is obstructed, the power of thought can conceive that which outstrips both thought and vision: an infinity that is in every way incommensurable with human existence, with its short successive "seasons."

It is not a question of atheism – which would maintain the place of the absent or negated god by replacing him with some other Reason (the sciences of the Enlightenment or a supreme Being) – but of the calm affirmation of both human existence and the universe's complete and utter contingency. This poem constitutes the first comprehensive assumption of that contingency. A contingency that has no room, need, or even notion of a god to slip in. Here we see how the affect is essential: the choice of sweetness and luxury over the anxiety and dread that would open the path to nihilism and its inverse, religiosity.

In his own reading of the poem, Bonnefoy opposes the musicality of Leopardi's language to the content (which is in his eyes devastating) of the poem itself. He comes quite close to interpreting the luxuriousness emanating from the poem as a consolation, or a delusion, that form offers thought. "Much of the form's beauty [...], should indeed have meaning, meaning for us, in even an empty universe [...]. Is this an infidelity to the very truth it contains?" The "ease" of Leopardi's words – it is not clear that this is the best qualifier for this language, which harbors an acerbity at the heart of its harmony, which cleaves to the organization of the phrase so as to go straight to what it says, as Vegliante's translation makes clear – somehow redresses the misfortune of which it speaks. To follow Bonnefoy in this way, I think, would be to engage in a profound misinterpretation, a betrayal, of what Leopardi is trying to formulate. A misunderstanding about Leopardi's vision of misfortune.

In many poems, Leopardi describes the destitution of human existence, caught between the pain of birth and the pain of death. Only early childhood, a season charged with intensity because it does not coincide with itself – being from the outset intoxicated with a promise, but delightful to remember – relieves this pain. In these youthful years:

> [...] the mean and bitter mystery of things
> Seems to brim with sweetness; when, spellbound,
> A boy will gaze like a raw young lover
> At his untried, untouched, untrustworthy life, his breath at that heavenly beauty
> He, in his own imagination, is creating.[2]

This is "a blessed season," a "very sweet state," and, if the hopes that take shape in it should turn out to be lies, they are nevertheless "delightful."

But even if one can always remember this singular time in their life (as when Leopardi returns to his father's garden, asking about the constellation, The Great Bear – I am alluding to the poem that struck me like a lightning bolt, and enabled my discovery of the poet, in the film by Visconti to which it gave its title: *Sandra ou Vaghe stelle dell'Orsa*,[3] it cannot, by itself, efface a more bitter truth:

> A man comes struggling into the world;
> His birth is in the shadow of death;
> Pain and suffering
> Are his first discoveries;
> And from that point
> His mother and his father try
> To console him for having been born.[4]

---

2. "Memories." trans. Eamon Grennan. in Leopardi: Selected Poems. Princeton: Princeton University Press, 1997, p. 43.

3. Released in English as *Sandra (Of a Thousand Delights)*.

4. "Night Song of a Nomadic Shepherd in Asia." trans. Eamon Grennan. Leopardi: Selected Poems. Princeton: Princeton University Press, 1997. p. 59.

The misfortune of man does not, however, stem from this originary condition. Its true cause is that he is constantly distracted from taking full stock of this condition. The world – be it the one that Leopardi frequented since his youth (the small town of Recanati, enclosed by lofty mountains), or be it cities like Rome, Florence, or Naples, which he would come to know – faults every intrepid exercise of thinking contingency, in favor of an idiotic confidence in the idea of progress, from which a new figure of religious meaning is drawn. And this obstinate backing, this frightened flight, before a thought that on the contrary should be the "dominant thought" of humanity, transforms each of these human worlds into so many fallacious and desolate deserts. If the poems dedicated to the moon are so beautiful, it is because the moon is the only one to whom the poem can address the solitude of this thought. She is indeed, in this sense, a "young girl," as Bonnefoy has him call her. But perhaps she is also the poet's "double": hence the couple she forms with the nomadic Asian shepherd who beholds and interrogates her. The nomadic shepherd's nakedness is a figure of mankind, of its essential nudity. The "silent moon," for its part, stands for the voice of the poet who addresses himself, from above, to this humanity that wanders in thought, buckling beneath the meaninglessness of both its own existence and that of the universe.

Leopardi's solitude thus results – let us not forget – from the corruption of his era: Leopardi – like Hölderlin, like Kleist ... – is caught in the terrible moment during which the admired, welcomed, and beloved revolutionary France, in the space of a few years, metamorphosed into an army that occupied and pillaged Europe, with Bonaparte as emperor. The new political era, which had barely been defined by the revolution, had turned back and retracted. And Italy folded in the face of invasion (just as Kleist's Prussia collaborated with the occupier). The confusion, the haunting and the horror of those years – tumultuously chronicled by Ippolito Nievo in his magnificent book, *Confessions of an Italian* – had marked Leopardi like a branding iron, as we can see from these lines from "On Dante's Monument":

O happy thou, whom Fate did not condemn
To live amid such horrors; who
Italian wives didst not behold
By ruffian troops embraced;
Nor cities plundered, fields laid waste
By hostile spear, and foreign rage;
Nor works divine of genius borne away
In sad captivity, beyond the Alps,
The roads encumbered with the precious prey;
Nor foreign rulers' insolence and pride;
Nor didst insulting voices hear,
Amidst the sound of chains and whips, [...]

In this conjuncture, whereupon, in the mouths of the French occupation, the "speech of freedom" has turned "impious," it will take a long time for Leopardi to find the path of a thought capable of holding together the contingency of the universe and the possibility of a collective and projected figure of humanity. His difficulty is that this figure cannot be linked to the figures of progress, or to any sort of historical teleology.

In "Palinode to Marchese Gino Capponi" (a sarcastic and visionary text that I cannot help but think acted as a leaven in Pessoa's creation of the poet, Alvaro de Campos), Leopardi outlines the new "Golden Age" that progress and the powerful promise to the world:

Universal love, railways,
the multiplicity of commerce, steam,
the printing press, and cholera unite,
the widely scattered peoples and climates [...]
Yet human happiness will be found in weightier
things, wholesome, not seen before. Our clothes
of wool or silk will become softer day by day.
Farmers and craftsmen hastening to throw off
rough garments, will hide their coarse skin in cotton,
and clothe their backs in beaver-furs.
Carpets, blankets, chairs, settees,
stools and dining tables, beds and other
kinds of furnishings will be more usable,
or at least easier on the eye, adorning
apartments with this month's beauty:

the wondrous kitchen will be ablaze
with new forms of pots and pans.
Journeys or rather flights will be
swifter than anyone dare imagine,
Paris to Calais, and London: London
to Liverpool [...] when hill and plain, I think,
and even the vast tracts of ocean,
will be covered by magazines,
the work of steam-driven presses
printing thousands of copies a second,
as if by a flight of cranes that suddenly
steals daylight from the broad landscape:
magazines, journals, the life and spirit
of the universe, sole fount of wisdom
for this age and all those to come!

This "joyous nineteenth century" will grow fat on unheard-of wars: "Nor will the generous race hold back its hand from blood, the blood of its own: Europe indeed [...]" and at any moment, will be "full of strife, whenever this crowd of brothers take the field against each other."

Would the century not, indeed, confirm Leopardi's lucid premonitions and end in the gigantic and criminal suicide that is the First World War?

The very last of Leopardi's poems, "The Broom," or "The Flower of the Desert," marks the invention of not only contingency's affect, but its courage as well. In order for mankind to undertake anything in unison, they must accept what, until now, the poet has only entertained with the silent and solitary moon: every human collective must rest upon a clear and lucid vision of the utter contingency of humanity and the universe.

To rally to this vision, the poem should begin by tearing down any idea that Nature is at the disposal of man – and substitute for this illusion a vision of Nature as entirely indifferent to man, thereby shattering every maternal representation. Modern man believes himself lord and master of the universe, when in reality he clings to an aleatory nook, which pays him no mind and blindly multiplies catastrophes that are well beyond his reckoning.

Only the acceptance that we exist entirely under the sign of contingency, like the desert flower, the broom, [*le genêt*] that accepts its destruction at the hands of the volcano so that it may then bloom again, can create a profound and non-fallacious love of men for each other. This love can no longer rest on any illusion of a meaningful universe with the presence of man at its center; nor can it rest on the belief in the fictions of religions and gods, but only on the naked truth of the utter absence of meaning. Just as the thought of the infinite has a luxurious sweetness as its affect, so the discreet perfume of the yellow flower subsisting in the volcanic deserts expresses the humble beauty of the collective figure into which humanity might project itself.

The apple, in the poem, that crushes the ant people, is clearly Newton's. This is why it makes sense to cite the *Zibaldone* here: "Science (enormously) augments knowledge, but does not increase the size of the ideas – to the contrary, it limits them. To know scientifically is not to grow spiritually."

The poem, and not science, is charged with humanity's spiritual growth, with making it able to confidently lean on the thought of contingency.

The vision that Leopardi develops in "The Broom" supposes that no figure of Evil can give birth to a transcendence. Likewise, the poem insists on the point that the destruction that menaces humanity is itself without meaning, that it obeys neither intention nor law. Its image is that of the blind path of lava down the side of an erupting volcano.

The notion of Evil is always in the service of reintroducing some sort of religiosity. The current religion of Nature ("Save our planet") is deployed for want of any older religion, sheltered even by the death of God, and it has its roots in a vision of Evil as the main sign of humanity. It lays the guilt for man's situation at his feet. Nature is threatened by man – the reverse of that torment from which Leopardi's poem seeks to deliver us. For him, there is a common struggle to be had *against* Nature, we must band together against her, no longer in a primitive, spontaneous gesture, but in a gesture that has been thought out, following a premeditated vision that would be solid and veracious knowledge. Moreover, let us understand that between man and the universe, there is neither oppressed nor oppressor. Or, to put it another way, there is no evil in the evil that survives. Contingency is beyond good and evil.

This poem thus shows that no eternity exists for man, so far as time as universe goes, a time that is, strictly speaking, not a time.

Nature (which is, ultimately, the Leopardian name for contingency) shall always have the last word on history. There is no progress, no possible triumphant march forward for humanity when everything can be annihilated in one blow, in one stroke. History and Nature (or, again, humanity and contingency) have nothing in common.

Nihilism, then? No. Nobility. Nobility is the name of the figure of love that Leopardi proposes to humanity: *to love oneself in a masterful thought of contingency*. This love is just as far from the Christian figure of love, whereby evil resides in man and requires the intervention of an external god who doles out evil as a test and takes it back upon himself, to palliate the disaster he inflicts on his creature. For Leopardi, it is a question of reuniting men in the courageous affirmation of a possible free common choice. The broom, happy with its desert, fills it with perfume.

The project that this poem deploys is consonant, rather, with the vast and burning question that occupies Jean-Luc Nancy in *Adoration*: is humanity capable of "*coming to grips with this: the world rests on nothing – and this is its keenest sense.*" Finding its confidence in this could be humanity's lot, if it is willing to conceive the earth as the meaningless place where it must live. The only place: "here."

How far we remain from inhabiting this place! Which shows to what extent Leopardi should still be useful for us!

By way of a conclusion

Just a couple of words concerning the category of poetry as a "supreme fiction" formalized by Stevens:

In various ways, the search for a nomination for the "earth" traverses the poetic propositions that I have just outlined. Each one of these poets cries out "Earth!" in order to announce something about which we have yet to have a common vision.

Each one of them is based within a world that comes after that which the gods inhabited. As Stevens notes, not only is "the death of one god [is] the death of all" (in "Notes Toward a Supreme Fiction"), but also "to see the gods dispersed into the air and dissolved like clouds is one of the great human experiences. It is not as if they had gone over the horizon to disappear for a time; nor as if they had been overcome by other gods of greater power and profounder knowledge. It is simply that they came to nothing."

How does this (irreversible) experience transform the nature of poetry itself? According to Stevens, from now on poetry must give life to "supreme fictions," without which we are incapable of representing this same life to ourselves. Furthermore, these fictions must present themselves as fictions. For these poets do not ask us to believe. This is precisely the task that Pessoa heartily takes up, not only within his invention of the heteronymic apparatus, but also when the orthonym proclaims, in one of his famous lines: "O poeta é um fingidor," that I translate as: "the poet is a fictioneer."

Thus poetry plays an essential role in the transformation of the category of truth; in its transformation, not its negation. It is striking that Jean-Luc Nancy's research also ends with the necessity of fiction: "in fiction, truth is not figured as if by impudent allegory: it is figured in so far as it is unfigurable. The infinite receives its finition, it opens within the finite." I revisit this theme on my own account with regard to the poem, to add this: the poem conceived as "a supreme fiction" undoes the lies of speech; language is the material of the poem; in it language is repudiated as both medium and instrument.

Thus poets can be:

Thinkers without final thoughts
In an always incipient cosmos
(Wallace Stevens, "July Mountain")

Afterward: questions of method

Today, what it means to read a poem has, to a certain degree, become vague. For this reason, I will state here what I mean by "to read a poem."

What had been conceived of in philosophy as the crisis or "end" of metaphysics has had a considerable effect on poetry. Deprived of an external speculative support, the poem has internalized its own vocation of thinking. It invented new operations within language where the relations between thought (poetry as thought) and the thought of this thought (poetry as thought *about poetry*) are directly at stake.

These original approaches of the poem, the production by way of the poem of immanent figures of thought requires, against the orientations of commentary and interpretation, a method – which will bear the name "reading."

Why does Mandelstam affirm that the poet is not haunted by desire but the fear of encountering a "concrete interlocutor," or worse still, "a friend in this century?" Because the poem, emerging out of nowhere, cuts straight into language. What the poem thinks is neither devoted nor calibrated. It is not tied down, it has wings. The poem-thought is a thought that one could say is absolute: absolute by way of its uprising, absolute in its enunciation.

Mandelstam's energetic refusal first of all requires the recognition that the poem exists and that we do not understand it, or not well, or too much, that in any case, nothing make us its privileged interlocutor. That it is as such does not mean that one must kneel down in front of Heidegger's resounding equation according to which we first of all need "men who are thinkers, in order for the speech of the poet to become perceptible." The Heideggerian subordination of the poet to the thinker does not have its origin within a failure of the poet; on the contrary, it expresses that the problem of the thinker has not been resolved. This thought of Being shielded from metaphysics that Heidegger fails to produce, he declares it should exist, unperceived, stored within the speech [*parole*] of the poets.

But what the poet needs is not a thinker from above. Rather what the poet needs is a reader, readers. A reader who always comes by chance. For the poem spreads from reader to reader. To say that the poem needs a reader or readers is to affirm that the thought of the poem is wholly within the poem itself. The poem is at once what it thinks and the dense, more or less compact, presentation of what it thinks. The poem is itself irreducible to its own presentation. This is the reason why we are never finished with a poem. Not because it offers up a polysemy of significations, or because it leaves a place for ambiguity and multiple meanings (except, of course, when it strives to do this deliberately), but because it says only one thing in the most precise manner available. It is to this unique thing, impossible to confuse with another, to which we feel compelled to return, until we are sure we have understood it.

No one reads a poem without being led to the apprenticeship of unlearning demanded by Alberto Caeiro. Here would be a good place to once again cite poem 46 from *The Keeper of Sheep*:

I try saying what I feel
Without thinking about what I feel.
I try fitting words to the idea
Without going down a corridor
Of thought to find words.

I don't always succeed in feeling what I know I should feel.
My thought swims the river only quite slowly,
Heavily burdened by clothes men have made it wear.

I try divesting myself of what I've learned,
I try to forget the mode of remembering they taught me,
And scrape off the ink they used to paint my senses,
Unpacking my true emotions,

Unwrapping myself, and being myself not Alberto Caeiro,
But a human animal that nature produced.

It is primarily a question of unlearning language and its figures.
The poem undermines all the figures identified by rhetoric. It undermines them because it substitutes for them what I propose
naming "figures of thought," singular each time within their entanglement with language. If we strive to name what is "there," if
we strive to go from these new figures back to the thought of the
poem, formal, rhetorical designations become confused. Thus, if
we encounter oxymorons in Pessoa, to state what they are and
what they are dealing with, we must designate them as "dialectical." If we want to identify the orthonym's use of negation and
double negation, they will have to be stated as "floating." Whereas
by all evidence, the tautology at work in Caeiro is enunciative and
not repetitive.

What then is reading when it is a question of reading poems?
The assertion that there is a question of method is not obvious.
Here the word "method" is used against the Heideggerian prob-
lematic of a "path toward the poem," homothetic with the idea
of the latter "advancing to the origin." The desire for a method
refers to the idea that the poem is the site of singular truth, that it
never illustrates anything from the outside, and that it states and
declares.

For this reason, no general proposition is possible; any thinking of a method has to be singularized regarding the several truths
the poem bears. But to affirm the necessity of a method is to opt
for the immanence of these truths in the poem. And to equally reject the hypothesis of a poem's "expressivity," concerning a
meaning or truth that would be external or anterior to it, as the
vision of the poem as pure language game – which, incidentally,
it might very well be. What is singular about the poem is that
speech, words, and immediately as a consequence, meanings,
constitute its material. But that speech is the poem's material – or
to put it another way, that every poem is a thought/relation on
speech – has a corollary: what it says does not correspond with the
meaning of the words already there.

The verse is only one of the possible demonstrations of this
non coincidence, by its long since proven capacity of shattering,
in creating a new unity of elocution, the unity of the signified

and meaning. To introduce into language a constant decentering between what is signified and what is thought, thought existing only as thought within the caesura of meaning, this is what the poem indefinitely strives for by any means. And from here we get its essential *obliqueness*.

Because of what has just been denoted as an intrinsic poetic obstacle, the consideration of the poem under the hypothesis that it is a thought requires the reader to be concerned about the poem's truth, by way of this "twice true" which is the singular mode in which a truth is presented in it.

What is this "twice true?" I borrow this category from Michel Deguy, who uses it to indicate, according to him, the constitutively "comparing" dimension of every poem. More broadly, if the poetic text must be said to be twice true, it is because it requires placing into tension two different enunciations that exist within the play of one within the other, without summoning any external referent. *What is shown* just as much as *what shows* is taken from one and the same linguistic material. In no way does the circuit refer to an outside, be it an eternal truth or reality.

Does this power of both isolation and production of the poem not demonstrate that the thought is found within the gap that separates the two enunciations? For it is within this gap that what Mallarme names "a third term, fusible and clear" emerges. To therefore privilege the gap of the "twice true," in designating it as "the indirect" of the poem, allows us to maintain that the poem does not consist of a to and fro between two truths but rather supports the short-circuiting of a truth. Thus it is the existence of this indirect that will call for a reading, what we name here as reading, and which obligates one to avoid commentary as much as interpretation.

Under these conditions, in order to grant the phrase "to read" its full scope and clarity, one must still posit that the poem's figures are not figures of speech. They are, and this is an original hypothesis, *figures of thought*. It is within the gap between saying and language – an effect of the violence from the former exerted upon the latter – that a "figure of thought" appears in the poem. The figure of thought is not a figure *of the thought*; nor is it a *thought formatted into figures*. It is a new element produced by the poem and it must be seized as such. Yet, grasping it requires a non-interpretative grasp of the poem. Once again, it would not be a question of grasping the "sense" of the poem, no more so than it would be a question of explaining its "meaning," one must grasp the "indirect" of the poem as the organizer in the poem of some figures of thought specific to it.

Each poem contains all that is needed within it. Each poem contains its own method.

List of the referenced poets and their works (in order of appearance)

Heinrich von Kleist
Anecdotes et petits écrits, Petite Bibliothèque Payot, 1981.
Théâtre complet, trad. Ruth Orthmann et Eloi Recoing, Babel, 2001.
Romantiques allemands, Gallimard, « La Pléiade », vol. i (*Nouvelles* : p. 1100-1341), 1963.

Alberto Caeiro
Fernando Pessoa, Obra poetica e em prosa, Lello & Irmao Editores, vol. i (p. 740-803), 1986.
Le Gardeur de troupeaux et les autres poèmes d'Alberto Caeiro, avec Poésies d'Alvaro de Campos, trad. Armand Guibert, NRF Poésie /Gallimard, 1987.
Fernando Pessoa, OEuvres poétiques, édition établie par Patrick Quillier, NRF/ Gallimard, « La Pléiade » (p. 6-86), 2001, trad. Michel Chandeigne, Maria Antonio Câmara Manuel et Patrick Quillier, révisée par ces deux derniers pour l'édition de « La Pléiade ».

Wallace Stevens
Collected Poetry and Prose, The Library of America, 1997.
Poèmes, trad. Marie-Jean Beraud-Villars et André Ravaute, introduction de Bernard Delvaille, Seghers, 1963.
Trois voyageurs regardent un lever de soleil (théâtre), trad. Leslie Kaplan et Claude Régy, Actes Sud-Papiers, 1988. Inclut une traduction de « Of Modern Poetry » par Nancy Blake et Hedi Kaddour.
L'homme à la guitare bleue, trad. Olivier Amiel, Éditions Michel Chandeigne, 1989.
Description sans domicile (bilingue), trad. Bernard Noël, Unes, 1989.
L'Aurore Boréale (bilingue), trad. Anne Luyat-Moore, Le Cri / In'Hui, 1995.
L'Ange nécessaire. Essais sur la réalité et l'imagination, trad. Sonia Bechka-Zouechtiagh et Claude Mouchard, Circé, 1997.
Esthétique du Mal, trad. Christian Calliyannis, in revue *Europe*, juin/ juillet 2000.
Idées de l'ordre (bilingue), trad. Claire Malroux, Atelier La Feugraie, 2000.
Harmonium (bilingue), trad. Claire Malroux, José Corti, 2002.
À l'instant de quitter la pièce /Le Rocher et derniers poèmes /Adagia (bilingue), trad. Claire Malroux, José Corti, 2006.

Osip Mandelstam
Entretien sur Dante, trad. Louis Martinez, L'Age d'homme, 1977.
Entretien sur Dante précédé de La pelisse, trad. Jean-Claude Schneider, La Dogana, 2002.
Pierre (édition de 1916), trad. Christian Mouze, Cazimi, 1997.
Tristia et autres poèmes, trad. François Kérel, NRF Poésie /Gallimard, 1982.
Le deuxième livre /1916-1925 (bilingue), trad. Henri Abril, Circé, 2002.
Les poèmes de Moscou /1930-1934 (bilingue), trad. Henri Abril, Circé, 2001.
Les Cahiers de Voronej /1935-1937 (bilingue), trad. Henri Abril, Circé, 1999.
Les Cahiers de Voronej (bilingue), trad. Christian Mouze, Harpo &, 2005.
Le bruit du temps, trad. Edith Scherrer, Seuil, « Points », 1988.
La quatrième prose, trad. Christian Mouze, Le Nyctalope, 1980.
La quatrième prose et autres textes, trad. André Markowicz, Christian Bourgois, 1993.
Voyage en Arménie, trad. Claude B. Levenson, L'Age d'homme, 1973.
Voyage en Arménie, trad. André du Bouchet, Mercure de France, 1984.

Physiologie de la lecture, trad. André du Bouchet, Fourbis, 1989.
La rage littéraire / récits, trad. Lily Denis, NRF/Gallimard, 1997.
Poèmes et essais (bilingue), trad. Christian Mouze, Alidades, 1987.
Vers du Soldat inconnu, trad. Yvan Mignot, coll. « La main courante » n° 27, 1991.
Simple promesse (choix de poèmes 1908-1937), trad. Philippe Jaccottet, Louis
    Martinez et Jean-Claude Schneider, La Dogana, 1994.
De la poésie, trad.Mayelasveta, Arcades /Gallimard, 1990.
Lettres, trad. Ghislaine Capogna-Bardet, Solin/Actes Sud, 2000.

Pier Paolo Pasolini

Bestemmia /Tutte le poesie (4 volumes en italien), Garzanti, 1996.
Poésies /1953-1964 (bilingue), trad. José Guidi, NRF Poésie /Gallimard, 1980.
Poèmes de jeunesse et quelques autres (bilingue), trad. Nathalie Castagné et Dominique
    Fernandez, NRF Poésie /Gallimard, 1995.
Dans le coeur d'un enfant (bilingue), traduit du frioulan par Vigji Scandella, Actes Sud, 2000.
Je suis vivant (bilingue), trad. Olivier Apert et Ivan Messac, Nous, 2001.
Qui je suis, trad. Jean-Pierre Milelli, Arléa, 1994.
Le dada du sonnet (bilingue), trad. Hervé Joubert-Laurencin, Les Solitaires Intempestifs, 2005.
Poésies /1943-1970, trad. Nathalie Castagné, René de Ceccatty, José Guidi et Jean-
    Charles Vegliante, NRF/Gallimard, 1990.
Correspondance générale / 1940-1975, trad. René de Ceccatty, NRF/Gallimard, 1991.

The "Misty" Poets

Bei Dao, Mang Ke, Yang Lian, Gu Cheng, Shu Ting, Ma Desheng, Jiang He, Yan Li,
Mo Fei, Duo Duo, Meng Lang, Chen Dong dong, Mo Mo, Hai Zi, Xi Chuan, Xiao
Kaiyu, Shu Cai, Zhu Zhu
Pour une présentation d'ensemble de ces poètes, il faut lire (en italien) le remarquable
    livre de Claudia Pozzana, *La poesia pensante. Inchieste sulla poesia cinese
    contemporanea*, Quodlibet Studio, 2010.
Poeti Cinesi contemporanei (bilingue chinois-italien), revue *In forma di parole* n° 3,
    trad. Claudia Pozzana et Alessandro Russo, Liviana Editrice, 1988.
Nuovi Poeti Cinesi (bilingue chinois-italien), dir. Claudia Pozzana et Alessandro
    Russo, Einaudi, 1996.
Un' altra Cina. Poeti e narratori degli anni Novanta (bilingue chinois-italien), revue
    In forma di parole, n° 1, 1999, dir. Claudia Pozzana et Alessandro Russo.
Bei Dao, *Speranza fredda* (bilingue chinois-italien), dir.Claudia Pozzana,Einaudi, 2003.
Quatre poètes chinois. BeiDao,Gu Cheng,Mang Ke, Yang Lian, trad.Chantal Chen-
    Andro et Annie Curien, avec la collaboration de François Dominique et Jean-
    Michel Rabaté, Cahier Ulysse fin de siècle n°27 / 28, Virgile, 1991.
Ma Desheng,*Vingt-quatre heures avant la rencontre avec le dieu de la mort* (bilingue),
    trad. Emmanuelle Péchenart, Actes Sud, 1992.
Ma Desheng, *Le portrait deMa*, Al Dante, 2010.
Bei Dao, *Au bord du ciel*, trad. Chantal Chen-Andro, Circé, 1994.
Bei Dao, Paysage au-dessus de zéro, trad. Chantal Chen-Andro, Circé, 2004.
Yang Lian, *La maison sur l'estuaire* (bilingue), trad. Chantal Chen-Andro, Maison
    des Écrivains Étrangers et des Traducteurs de Saint-Nazaire, 2001.
Yang Lian, *Masques et crocodiles*, trad.Chantal Chen-Andro,Virgile, coll. « Ulysse
    fin de siècle », 2002.
Yang Lian, *Là où s'arrête la mer*, Caractères, 2004.

Yang Lian, *Notes manuscrites d'un diable heureux*, Caractères, 2010.

Yang Lian, *Tenebre /Darknesses, La casa delle ombre / House like shadow* (trilingue chinois-italien-anglais), in *PlayOn Poetry*, dir. Jacopo Ricciardi, 2002.

Yang Lian, *Dove si ferma il mare /Where the sea stands still* (trilingue chinois-italien-aglais), dir. Claudia Pozzana, Libri Scheiwiller, coll. « PlayOn », 2004.

Yang Lian, *Non-person singular* (bilingue chinois-anglais), trad. BrianHolton, The Well Sweep Press, 1994.

Yang Lian, *Where the Sea Stands Still /New poems* (bilingue chinois-anglais), trad. Brian Holton, Bloodaxe Books, 1999.

Yang Lian, *Notes of a Blissful Ghost*, trad. Brian Holton, Renditions Paperbacks, 2002.

Yang Lian, *Yi* (bilingue chinois-anglais), trad. Mabel Lee, Green Integer 35, 2002.

Yang Lian, *Concentric Circles*, trad. Brian Holton et Agnès Hung-Chong Chan, Bloodaxes Books, 2005.

Yang Lian, *Unreal City. Selection of poems and proses about Auckland*, Auckland University Press, 2006.

Yang Lian, *Riding Pisces. Poems from 5 collections* (bilingue chinois-anglais), trad. Brian Holton, Shearmans Books, 2008.

Yang Lian, *Lee Valley Poems*, Bloodaxe Books, 2009.

Gennadiy Aygi

Léon Robel, *Aïgui*, Seghers, coll. « Poètes d'aujourd'hui », 1993.

Degré : de stabilité, trad. Léon Robel, Seghers / Laffont, coll. « Change », 1976.

Festivités d'hiver, trad. Léon Robel, Les Éditeurs Français réunis, 1978.

Sommeil Poésie Poèmes, trad. Léon Robel, Seghers, 1984.

Le Cahier de Véronique / Les six premiers mois de ma fille (bilingue), trad. Léon Robel, Le Nouveau Commerce, 1984.

Le temps des ravins / 1982-1984 (bilingue), trad. Léon Robel, Le Nouveau Commerce, 1990.

L'enfant-la rose (bilingue), trad. AndréMarkowicz, Le Nouveau Commerce, 1992.

Hors-commerce Aigui, textes réunis et traduits par AndréMarkowicz, Le Nouveau Commerce, 1993.

Conversations à distance, trad. Léon Robel, Circé, 1994.

Toujours plus loin dans les neiges (bilingue), trad. Léon Robel, Obsidiane, 2005.

Gennady Aygi, *Selected Poems 1954-1994* (bilingue russe-anglais), trad. Peter France, Angel Books, 1997.

Gennady Aygi, *Child-and-Rose*, trad. Peter France, avec une préface de Bei Dao, New Directions Books, 2003.

Giacomo Leopardi

Canti, trad. François-Alphonse Aulard, Juliette Bertrand, Philippe Jaccottet et Georges Nicole, NRF Poésie /Gallimard, 1999.

OEuvres, oeuvres en prose traduites par Juliette Bertrand, poèmes traduits par François-Alphonse Aulard, Philippe Jaccottet et Georges Nicole, avec une préface de Giuseppe Ungaretti, Collection UNESCO d'oeuvres représentatives, Éditions Mondiales, 1964.

« Giacomo Leopardi », revue *Europe*, juin-juillet 1998, avec 4 traductions de Jean-Charles Vegliante : « L'infini », « Le soir du jour de fête », « À la lune », « Fragment (Terreur nocturne) ».

Keats et Leopardi. Quelques traductions nouvelles (bilingue), trad. Yves Bonnefoy, Mercure de France, 2000.

Judith Balso: studies on poems and poets

« Les Pessoas-livros » in La politique des poètes, sous la responsabilité de Jacque Rancière, Bibliothèque du Collège International de Philosophie, Albin Michel, 1992.

« Pessoa : nous reconstruire, sans idéal ni espérance » in Artistes et philosophes : éducateurs ?, Éditions du Centre Georges Pompidou, 1994.

« Pasolini, l'incivile éclaircie » in revue Barca, n°5, nov. 1995.

« Le Paradoxe du Traducteur : hommage à Armand Guibert » in Quadrant (revue d'études lusitano-brésiliennes du Centre de recherche en Littérature de Langue Portugaise de l'Université Paul-Valéry deMontpellier iii), n°16, 1999.

« L'hétéronymie : une métaphysique sans métaphysique » in Pessoa :Unité,Diversité, Obliquité (Actes du Colloque Pessoa de Cerisy), Bourgois, 2000.

« De la poésie sévère » in revue Dédales, n°11 et 12, automne-hiver 2000.

« Le poème, part de la chose même et non à son propos—un parallèle Pessoa/Stevens » in revue Amastra-N-Gallar, n°3, printemps 2002.

« Actualité de Dante » in revue Amastra-N-Gallar, n°4, automne 2002.

« Ricardo Reis, l'effaceur des dieux » in revue Contre Jour /Cahiers Littéraires n°5, 2004.

« Armand Guibert, inventeur de Pessoa » in Lisbonne, atelier du lusitanisme français, études réunies par Jacqueline Penjon et Pierre Rivas, Presses Sorbonne nouvelle, 2005.

Working translation of « Notes Toward a Supreme Fiction » by Wallace Stevens in collaboration with Andrew Gibson (2005), unpublished.

« Aïgui, le poète sans particularités » in revue Amastra-N-Gallar, n°13, hiver 2007.

« The Necessary Truth : About Jan Zwicky » in revue Poïesis, n°9, 2007.

Pessoa, le passeur métaphysique Seuil, 2006.

« Pessoa, le sujet inachevé » Conférence prononcée dans le cadre du Centre de recherches « Littérature et poétique comparées » de l'Université Paris x Nanterre, sur l'invitation de Camille Dumoulié (http://www.revuesilene.com/f/index. php?sp=liv&livre_id=118).

« Léger, allant de l'avant, choisissant toujours la vie, la jeunesse » in Europe, n°947, « Pasolini », mars 2008.

« Poème : relire » (à propos de l'oeuvre poétique de Philippe Beck) (2010) à paraître dans la revue Il particolare.

« Atalante et Hippomène—sur la fonction singulière de la poésie dans la philosophie d'Alain Badiou » (2010) intervention aux « Journées Alain Badiou ».

« Armand Guibert, la traduction comme voyage » (2010), Armand Guibert, poète, éditeur, traducteur, sous la direction de Guy Dugas.

« Owl's Clover » by Wallace Stevens, Working translation into French in collaboration with Andrew Gibson (incomplete).

Univocal Publishing
123 North 3rd Street, #202
Minneapolis, MN 55401
www.univocalpublishing.com

ISBN 9781937561178

Jason Wagner, Drew S. Burk
(Editors)
All materials were printed and bound
in July 2014 at Univocal's atelier
in Minneapolis, USA.

This work was composed in Garamond and Gill Sans
The paper is Mohawk Via, Pure White Linen.
The letterpress cover was printed
on Crane's Lettra Fluorescent.
Both are archival quality and acid-free.